Children of the Universe
Cosmic Education in the Montessori Elementary Classroom

By

Michael and D'Neil Duffy

Illustrated by

Amber Amann

With an Introduction by

Aline D. Wolf

Parent Child Press
A division of Montessori Services
www.MontessoriServices.com

Copyright © 2002, 2014 Michael Duffy and D'Neil Duffy. All rights reserved.

Library of Congress Control Number: 2013922911

ISBN 978-0-939195-43-5

No part of this book may be used or reproduced in any manner whatsoever without written permission from the publisher except in the case of brief quotations embodied in critical articles and reviews.

From the New Publisher

In June 2013 Parent Child Press became part of Montessori Services. This reprint of Michael and D'Neil Duffy's *Children of the Universe* was one of our first projects. This new edition includes updated material, as well as updated website references.

Since its first printing in 2002, *Children of the Universe* has become a standard reference and/or required reading for many Montessori elementary training courses. Although the Duffys' extensive explanation of Montessori's Cosmic Education could never replace Montessori elementary training, it is a valuable resource for anyone seeking to understand the foundation of the Montessori philosophy for the elementary years. Readers will gain much insight and inspiration from this comprehensive resource.

It is a privilege to continue the work of Parent Child Press and, specifically, to support the Duffys' contribution to the Montessori world.

Jane Campbell
Founder
Montessori Services

Dedicated to

our daughter, Mignon, and our son, Brett,

whose schooling introduced us to Montessori,

and to all the children we have taught over the years.

Acknowledgements

We acknowledge, first of all, the contribution of Aline Wolf to this book. A respected author of many interpretations of Montessori, particularly the place of spirituality in Montessori's ideas, she is someone whose wisdom has contributed to our own understanding of the essence of Montessori. She has offered her valuable insights as the primary editor of the various drafts of this book.

We offer our gratitude to Grazia Francesca Honneger, a leading Montessori educator in Italy who asked us to give a presentation on Cosmic Education at an international conference in Rome in 1996. That lecture formed the basis of another talk that attracted the attention of Aline Wolf in 1999.

We also thank those who graciously agreed to read the manuscript of this book and whose comments helped us to improve the final product, particularly Kim McMaken, Mignon Duffy, Stephanie Miles, Catherine Maresca, Dr. Margaret Loeffler, Gail Maatman, and Gerald Wolf.

Our gratitude also goes to Amber Amann, a former student at our school and a graphic artist by profession, whose interpretive illustrations grace this text. For the photos, we thank the students and teachers at Blackstock Montessori School, as well as Laura Earnest, the photographer.

In addition, we want to acknowledge the work of Carole Korngold, founder and prime mover of the Center for Montessori Teacher Education in New York, as well as all our colleagues at CMTE/NY for the years of guidance and inspiration that made this book possible.

Table of Contents

Introduction—Aline D. Wolf ... vi

Foreword ... viii

Chapter 1—Cosmic Education: What It Is and Why We Teach It ... 1

Chapter 2—Evolution and Cosmic Education ... 13

Chapter 3—Cosmic Education and the Cultural Curriculum ... 29

Chapter 4—The Story of the Universe ... 43

Chapter 5—The Story of the Solar System ... 61

Chapter 6—The Story of the Earth ... 73

Chapter 7—The Story of Life ... 83

Chapter 8—The Story of Humans ... 101

Chapter 9—The Story of Civilizations ... 117

Chapter 10—Cosmic Education and the Future ... 131

Appendices:

   Scope and Sequence ... 145

   Classroom Resources ... 151

   Glossary ... 189

   References ... 201

About the Authors ... 204

Introduction

Since it was formulated by Maria Montessori in the 1940s, Cosmic Education has been somewhat of a mystery in the academic milieu. The two words are not combined in dictionaries, or in encyclopedias, and until now there has been no book that details this curriculum for inquiring readers.

Taking a clue from the word "cosmic," some individuals have mistakenly interpreted it to mean simply a study of astronomy. Others guessed it had something to do with space explorations. Only those who were enrolled in Montessori teacher-training courses were aware of Cosmic Education as an all-inclusive six-year curriculum for elementary-age children. This challenging program relates all academic subjects to each other, demonstrates the oneness of all creation and, most importantly, places children's primary orientation to life firmly in the universe.

In his book *The Hidden Heart of the Cosmos*, Brian Swimme declares that cosmology is a wisdom tradition. It draws on science for the gathering of facts and theories, but its power is to awaken those deep convictions that are necessary for wisdom.[1]

His words affirm what Maria Montessori wrote fifty years earlier in *The Absorbent Mind*: "So in the child, besides the vital impulse to create himself or herself, there must be yet another purpose, a duty to fulfill in harmony with the universe, something to do in the service of the united whole."[2] By stretching their intelligence and imagination into the universe itself, Montessori believed that Cosmic Education could help children understand themselves as human beings and live according to the wisdom of the universe.

What could be more important now in America where children's lives are caught up in consuming products dictated by non-stop advertising and in imitating models ordained by the all-powerful commercial media?

In a lecture I heard recently, the historian Thomas Cahill, said, "The worst feature of today's world is that people are locked up in themselves." This preoccupation with self, I believe, includes individuals of all ages, corporations, and governments. It is the tragic flaw that seriously limits today's students, causes unethical business practices, and feeds the arrogance

---

1 Brian Swimme (1996), *The Hidden Heart of the Cosmos*. Maryknoll, NY: Orbis Books, p. 31 and p. 101.

2 Maria Montessori (published in U.S. 1967), *The Absorbent Mind*. New York: Dell Publishing Co. Inc., p. 239.

of political leaders who promote their own or their country's economic interests at the expense of the environment and of other less fortunate countries.

What can save us from this destructive preoccupation with self? "We need to open our hearts to others like a never-failing stream," Cahill urged in his lecture.

Such a radical change of heart can come about only through an education that proclaims to children in their most impressionable years that the universe is a web of relationships. If we are to survive, self-interest must give way to the common good, over-consumption must fade into moderation, and businesses and governments must operate with universal values rather than with self-serving principles.

Not this book, nor any other single book, can accomplish such a reform. I believe, however, that Cosmic Education, detailed here, can introduce elementary-age children to the universal values that can save us from wars and planetary destruction.

Cosmic Education is a first step in gaining this lofty but indispensable view of life. In *Nurturing the Spirit in Non-Sectarian Classrooms* I wrote, "The value of cosmic education, as I see it, is that it places the child's life in a spiritual perspective. No one can be confronted with the cosmic miracle and not see that there is more to life than our everyday experiences. Fast foods, designer sneakers, video games and sports heroes all pale beside the wonder of the universe."

I am delighted that Michael and D'Neil Duffy, both experienced Montessori educators, undertook the formidable task of detailing this extensive curriculum. They did it well, never failing to relate elementary level astronomy, physics, chemistry, geology, geography, biology, archeology, and history to the unity of all things in the universe.

Reading their manuscript was an exciting learning experience for me. My purpose in publishing it is to bring home to teachers the importance of helping elementary-age students to see themselves, not as self-engrossed individuals, but as Children of the Universe with all that this image entails.

Aline D. Wolf
Spring 2002

Foreword

This book is an exploration of Cosmic Education, which is the heart of the Montessori elementary curriculum. By emphasizing the oneness of everything in the Universe, this all-embracing curriculum fosters not only well-educated students but children who have a unique understanding of themselves and the world around them. This six-year Montessori experience gives elementary students opportunities to appreciate their roots in the Universe, to sense their place in its context, and to embrace the role this defines for their lives.

Cosmic Education is the unifying element of the curriculum for the elementary-age child, providing the conceptual framework for all the scientific and cultural subjects. Its greatest value, however, may lie in the appropriate way it meets the developmental needs of six- to twelve-year-old students — capturing their imagination, piquing their curiosity, capitalizing on their desire to move beyond their earlier environment, and wrestling with their constant questions of "How?" and "Why?"

This is not a how-to book for either teachers or parents, but it can be relevant to both. For Montessori teachers, already trained in the cosmic curriculum, this book can reinforce the importance of Cosmic Education in their vocational mission and serve as a stimulus for exploring new information in light of modern scientific discoveries. Most importantly, it can serve as a synthesis — helping them to constantly relate all parts of the curriculum to the all-important "whole." In addition, this book can serve non-Montessori teachers as a vehicle for opening a much-needed dialogue for any educators seeking a more timely approach to the 21st century.

This volume can also be useful to parents of Montessori students who are often baffled by the words "Cosmic Education." This book can not only help them to understand the rationale for offering this unique curriculum to their children, but it can stimulate conversations and activities at home that will complement the cosmic ideals.

Maria Montessori outlined her overall plan for Cosmic Education in her slim volume *To Educate the Human Potential* and elaborated on it in *From Childhood to Adolescence* and in some of her other writings and lectures. Her insights in these sources are brilliant, but the details are sparse. So in order to implement Cosmic Education, training courses have relied on the work of Montessori followers and these procedures are duly recorded in the albums of every trainee. In various training courses over the course of many years, some different nomenclature and types of stories have evolved. We believe, though, that the essence of Cosmic Education is the same for all Montessori educators, no matter what terms they use or what affiliation they may have.

In this first book to give a comprehensive view of Cosmic Education within the broad scope of the elementary curriculum, our goal is to give new life to the subject, to emphasize its importance, and to stimulate discussion at all levels of Montessori education. It is our hope that a resurgence of interest in this powerful curriculum can lead us all to a more peaceful future.

Michael Duffy
D'Neil Duffy
Spring 2002

Cosmic Education:
What It Is and Why We Teach It

Chapter 1

Cosmic Education: What It Is and Why We Teach It

In the United States and in many other countries of the world, "Montessori education" has become a household term to describe schools with a special approach to the education of young children. Even though many Montessori schools now include the elementary years, relatively little is known about the essence of this curriculum. Parents of Montessori students themselves are at times mystified by what is being offered to their children. Even those who teach in Montessori schools sometimes lose sight of its guiding principles.

"Cosmic Education" is the foundation for the entire Montessori elementary curriculum, especially through studies of history and biology, as well as related subjects such as geography, physical science, and chemistry. In order to understand the essence of Cosmic Education, it is important to know where it comes from, what it is, and why it is used to teach elementary children. These three questions form a pattern that will become familiar throughout this book; they relate to past, present, and future—the origin or roots of Cosmic Education, how we define it in the present, and what it offers to the future of the children we teach.

Maria Montessori (1870–1952), the founder of this worldwide educational methodology, began her professional life as a physician, one of the first female doctors in Italy. After becoming involved in the medical care of children with special problems, she began designing hands-on learning materials for them. Because of the remarkable success she had with these children, Montessori became determined to use similar methods for children without handicaps or disabilities. Education gradually supplanted medicine as her career. When she opened her first "Children's House" in 1907 in one of the poorest neighborhoods of Rome, she embarked on a path that would shape the rest of her life's work and bring her international fame, from Europe to Asia to the Americas, through her innovative approach to the education of young children.[1]

Her 1911 visit to the United States brought a promising start to Montessori education here. World War I, however, disrupted the training of teachers, and disagreements with the Alexander Graham Bells and other distinguished sponsors led to the temporary demise of the method in this country until its revival in the early 1960s. Since then, thousands of private Montessori schools have been established in the United States, and hundreds of public schools have adopted the method as well.[2]

Maria Montessori spent most of her life developing an educational method for the early childhood years. It was only toward the end of her life that she expanded to the elementary level and developed her ideas on Cosmic Education.

Montessori's approach, we believe, can be an effective educational method for elementary-age children in the new millennium in America and throughout the world. Even more, it can be a catalyst for peace in the world and for the preservation of our species and our planet. However, to accomplish these lofty goals, it must be understood as something more than a novel set of learning materials. It is necessary to probe and understand Cosmic Education, the philosophy which underlies the Montessori elementary program.

---

1 Two excellent biographies of Maria Montessori are E. M. Standing's classic *Maria Montessori: Her Life and Work*, New York, New American Library, 1957, and Rita Kramer's *Maria Montessori, a Biography*, Chicago, University of Chicago Press, 1976.

2 Two sources of further information about Montessori in America are a collection of articles called *Montessori in Contemporary American Culture*, Portsmouth, NH, Heinemann, 1992, particularly the chapter by Nancy McCormick Rambusch, "Montessori in America: A History;" and John Chattin-McNichols's book *The Montessori Controversy*, Albany, NY, Delmar Publishers, 1992.

The Origins of Cosmic Education

Cosmic Education, the hope of a peaceful future, was the offspring of a wartime experience. Maria Montessori and her son, Mario Montessori, had been lecturing and working in India at the time of the outbreak of World War II. As Italian citizens, they were put under a form of house arrest by the British government for the duration of the war. It was during that time, which has come to be known as the Kodaikanal experience, that the underlying philosophy of Cosmic Education was developed.

Mario Montessori recounts that it was only through that period of forced retirement that he and his famous mother were able to find the time to expand her educational system and develop the principles of the infant-toddler level at one end of the spectrum and the elementary level at the other.[3]

Maria Montessori was 70 years old in 1940, and her schools had been closed in countries sympathetic to Nazism and fascism. Mario, the out-of-wedlock son who had been hidden from public view during his mother's early professional life in Italy, had by then become a close collaborator and what he himself called a "devoted apostle" who accompanied his mother to lectures and training courses.

India, which as a British colony was on the side of the Allies, put the Montessoris in a form of internment, treating them as "enemy aliens," something Mario found to be "ludicrous to say the least."[4] However, because of the stature and prestige of Maria Montessori, they were allowed to leave Madras and live out those years in a more mountainous and pastoral region called Kodaikanal.[5] It was through this experience of nature, working with children, and taking time for reflection, that the two of them were able to develop the philosophy of Cosmic Education.

The Montessoris had gone to India to lecture and train teachers as guests of the Theosophical Society. According to their Internet web page, the Theosophical Society, founded in 1875, is a worldwide body whose primary object is Universal Brotherhood without distinction based on the realization that

---

[3] Mario Montessori (1998), "The Impact of India," *The NAMTA Journal*, Vol. 23 (2), Spring, p. 28. Reprint of an article that first appeared in the 1969/70 issue of *Around the Child*, the publication of the Association of Montessorians—Calcutta.

[4] Ibid., p. 27.

[5] David Kahn (1998), "The Kodaikanal Experience: Kahn–Montessori Interview," *The NAMTA Journal*, Vol. 23 (2), Spring, p. 35. Reprint of an article that first appeared in the *NAMTA Quarterly* Fall 1979.

life, and all its diverse forms, human and non-human, is indivisibly One.⁶ Its world headquarters is located in Madras, India. It doesn't take a lot of imagination to assume that the development of Cosmic Education certainly was influenced by the Montessoris' contact with this organization in India.

While Maria Montessori remained committed to her native religion of Roman Catholicism throughout her life, she also was open to the insights of other religious traditions. In India, Mario Montessori recalls that he and his mother "had the privilege of coming in prolonged contact with children in all situations, whether they belonged to communities of Brahmins or of Parsis; of Buddhists, Christians, Hindus, Muslims, or Zoroastrians."⁷ The predominance of the Eastern-style religions of India and their sensitivity to the spiritual unity and harmony of the Universe is certainly another factor in explaining the origins of Cosmic Education.

The Nature of Cosmic Education

The goal of Cosmic Education is to guide the child toward an initial examination of the question "Who am I?" This seemingly simple question is actually one of the most profound metaphysical questions we can pose about the nature of life and self.

If a child ponders this query, his first answer is likely to be his name. With a little coaxing, he might add that he is a boy, an American, a Boy Scout, a soccer player, etc. But there are hundreds, even thousands, of others who meet this description, even down to the name. What makes this child different or special?

The child's answers are the beginnings of a search for an identity, something to define who the child really is as a member of the human species and as an individual apart from everyone else in the world. They are an attempt to capture the individual at the present moment of time. This attempt to define the child is intimately joined with two other aspects of the child's identity, representing the past and the future.

The "Who am I?" question is really three questions in one. The other two parts of the question are "Where do I come from?" and "Why am I here?"

---

6   www.ts-adyar.org

7   Mario Montessori, op. cit., p. 29.

(or "Where am I going?"). The first of these, which relates to the child's past, constitutes part of his present identity in the form of ontological and historical memory, or what Montessori referred to as "mneme."[8] It is the part of identity that comes from ancestry in the broadest sense of that term. The latter question, which relates to the child's future, makes up part of his identity in the form of a life-related goal or contribution to the Universe, what Montessori referred to as a "cosmic task." This is connected to "horme,"[9] or the vital urge of evolutionary survival. It is the part of identity that comes from the contribution a child—as a member of the human species and as a unique individual—can make to the preservation and betterment of the world.

The two additional questions—"Where do I come from?" and "Why am I here?"—are nothing more than an elaboration on the more basic and all-inclusive question: "Who am I?" Whenever we refer to this single question in the rest of the book, it should be understood to carry with it all the connotations of the broader understanding of the question as outlined above.

The "Who am I?" question, in all three of its aspects, can be approached on the level of the human species, trying to find the place of our particular species within the evolutionary flow of life on our planet—past, present, and future. Or it can be approached on the level of the individual person, trying to find what contribution each of us can make to the cosmic task of the whole species. The two levels co-exist and interact constantly within the Montessori curriculum and within each child.

Maria Montessori explored the concept of a "cosmic task" by telling stories. One of her favorites was centered around the drama of the oceans, the birthplace of life on Earth, which were at the same time the recipient of tons of minerals dissolved by water and washed into the seas. As calcium carbonates and other minerals threatened to poison the burgeoning life forms before they had a chance to establish themselves, the now-extinct trilobites, then the cephalopods and crinoids, and finally the corals, took it upon themselves to capture certain minerals and transform them into pieces of themselves, thus rescuing the oceans from fatal pollution. Instead of life being destroyed, the tiny corals built these minerals into chains of

---

8   Maria Montessori, *To Educate the Human Potential* (first published in 1948), p. 20.
9   Ibid., p. 21.

mountains under the sea.[10] Just as water has the cosmic task of dissolving the minerals and carrying them to the oceans, the corals have the job of transforming those minerals into beautiful reefs and even massive islands. This is the cosmic task of corals, the contribution of these tiny creatures to the Universe.

Mario Montessori Jr., a professional psychologist who has maintained an interest in the Montessori movement, explains his grandmother's ideas about the cosmic task in this way: "Her ultimate explanation of this task as a finality, intended by creation to maintain the cosmic order in nature, belongs to her personal philosophy and need not be accepted by all. But the phenomena to which she alludes in explaining it are observable and belong to the natural order of things. Today this is referred to as the natural equilibrium."[11]

Cosmic Education is intended to help each of us search for our cosmic task as a species and as individuals. To do this, we must understand ourselves in context. It is only against the background of our place in the Universe, our relationship to other living organisms, and our understanding of human unity within cultural diversity, that we can attempt to answer the question "Who am I?"

There are more complicated definitions of Cosmic Education that we could include in this discussion. In fact, Camillo Grazzini, co-director of the AMI (Association Montessori Internationale) teacher training center in Bergamo, Italy, felt the need to formulate six separate statements to attempt to capture the full essence of the words. These statements relate to (1) a unitary vision of the world, (2) a knowledge of the Universe as an organizing force, (3) an appreciation of interdependency, (4) an awareness of a cosmic task, (5) humanity's experience of a new way of life, and (6) a pedagogy that passes from whole to detail.[12] For the purposes of this book, we will focus on the simple approach outlined above of asking "Who am I?" with the child, an approach which we believe leads by implication to all the meanings listed by Grazzini.

---

10 Ibid., p. 35 ff.

11 Mario M. Montessori, Jr., *Education for Human Development: Understanding Montessori*, p. 100.

12 Camillo Grazzini (1997), "Cosmic Education at the Elementary Level and the Role of the Materials," *The NAMTA Journal*, Vol. 22 (1), Winter, p.50. Reprinted from "The Child, the Family and the Future," proceedings of the AMI conference in Washington in 1994.

Certainly there is no single answer to that question, no set of statements that will answer it exhaustively. Each attempt at an answer is only a partial response. It can never satisfy us to the point that we would want to discontinue our search. The search is a lifelong one, and we can hope only to approach the mystery of our own existence without ever solving it completely.

Is Cosmic Education Appropriate for Elementary Children?

Are elementary-age children really capable of exploring this kind of a philosophical question? Do they have the mental capacity and level of life experience necessary to pursue such a profound search? Maria Montessori thought so.

She believed that the child of six to twelve years of age could be properly educated only in the context of the whole of reality. She saw the child in this stage of development as reaching out to the world, indeed beyond our own tiny world to the immensity of the Universe itself. She based this on the way she came to understand child development as she observed children with the trained eye of a physician/scientist.

Montessori divided the pathway to adulthood into four major stages or planes of development. In the first plane, from birth to about the age of six, children are in the stage of the "absorbent mind" when they take in knowledge from the environment around them without fully conscious intent. In the second plane, from about age six to twelve, children enter into society and, through the power of the imagination, expand their circle of consciousness to the world. In the third plane, from age 12 to 18, children go through adolescence, exploring areas of interest in more depth and making choices that will determine their future.[13] In the fourth plane, from 18 to 24, the young adult moves into full maturity.[14] We focus on the second plane in this book.

Montessori described the second plane of development as a break from the period that went before it: "Psychologically there is a decided change

---

13 Maria Montessori, *From Childhood to Adolescence* (first published in 1948).

14 Paula Polk Lillard, *Montessori Today: A Comprehensive Approach to Education from Birth to Adulthood*, p. 5 ff.

in personality, and we recognize that nature has made this a period for the acquisition of culture, just as the former was for the absorption of the environment."[15]

Montessori identified several key characteristics of the child in the second plane of development that amount to a metamorphosis or separation from the first plane. First, "the child needs wider boundaries for social experiences;"[16] second, the child undergoes a "passage from the sensorial, material level to the abstract;"[17] and third, there is "a turning toward the intellectual and moral sides of life."[18] All three of these developmental characteristics indicate that the elementary-age child has a need for Cosmic Education.

The first characteristic, the need for wider boundaries or opportunities, is explained by Montessori as the need to "go out."[19] Children in the second plane of development are no longer content to remain inside their homes and schools, or to limit their experience to what they feel inside themselves. They have become aware of the world outside. They begin to interact in a more social way with each other. Instead of the side-by-side activity we have become accustomed to seeing in younger children, they enter a stage of development where they actually work together. They need field trips and excursions to give them an experience of the world outside their own limited surroundings. "Going out" is a catchall phrase for the whole phenomenon of widening horizons experienced by the child in this stage of development.

If children in this second plane need to "go out," there is nothing to say that there should be conceptual boundaries on that going out. Certainly, safety and practicality impose limitations on the extent of actual excursions, but the child is opening up to a virtually limitless quest into the world outside herself. Cosmic Education addresses the broad scope of that outward journey into all of reality.

The second characteristic, the passage to abstraction, is something we all recognize in children. From the earlier "what" questions, seeking names for everything they experience concretely, children now pass to a "why" stage, asking the reason for everything they can experience or imagine abstractly. It

---

15   Maria Montessori, *To Educate*, p. 4.

16   Maria Montessori, *From Childhood*, p. 3.

17   Ibid., p. 5.

18   Ibid., p. 5.

19   Ibid., p. 12.

is through the remarkable power of the human imagination that Montessori believes children are able to enter into contact with what they have not been able to experience directly.[20]

This power of imagination and the ability to abstract from what they know concretely means that children are not limited in their search for knowledge—the Universe itself is the limit. As part of Cosmic Education, Montessori believed that the intelligence and imaginative powers of children should stretch out into the farthest reaches of the Universe in order to understand themselves as human beings and to discover their cosmic task.

The third characteristic is a new level of moral development. Many philosophers and psychologists have agreed with Montessori that this begins around the age of six or seven. Children at this age are developing a conscience, the ability to distinguish between right and wrong, apart from the directives of the adults around them. They begin to make claims of "fairness" that indicate an ability to recognize universal imperatives beyond their own needs and wants, even if they are only in the early stages of this development.[21]

Cosmic Education contributes to this moral development. What moral imperative is more basic than meeting the "cosmic task" of our species and of each of us as individuals? Cosmic Education helps young students discover the moral imperative by which they should live their lives. The human race, and every individual within it, has a cosmic task, a place in the Universe, a job to accomplish for the benefit of the cosmos.

These developmental changes in the child of six to twelve years old create a new educational framework for Montessori. "Let us give him a vision of the whole universe," she urges us. Presenting the Universe to the child allows the child to focus learning and to organize knowledge. "No matter what we touch, an atom, or a cell, we cannot explain it without knowledge of the wide universe."[22]

Montessori certainly did not claim that elementary-age children can adequately answer the "Who am I?" question—any more than we can as

---

20 Ibid., p. 17–23.

21 For a deeper discussion of a child's moral development, see Robert Coles's *The Moral Intelligence of Children*, 1997. Ironically, this book was published in the same year of republication of Jean Piaget's classic book, *The Moral Judgment of the Child*, New York: Free Press.

22 Maria Montessori, *To Educate*, p. 8–9.

adults. However, why prevent them from beginning the exploration as soon as they can? The characteristics of children at this age suggest that now is the time to begin, that this is the "sensitive period" to implant the initial impressions on which a lifetime search for meaning can be based.

If we follow Montessori's theory of sensitive periods as laid out in her pedagogy, the elementary age is the sensitive period for Cosmic Education. This is the easiest time in the child's life to begin Cosmic Education, just as the early years are the sensitive period for learning to speak and therefore the easiest time for a child to acquire a first and second language. It is not impossible to postpone that learning until later in life, but we do so at the risk of making that learning difficult for the child instead of a joy. The elementary age is the ideal time in life to help a child develop the mindset and context for asking the "Who am I?" question. This is the time to introduce all children to a quest that they can pursue for their entire lives.

Montessori warned against the postponement of introducing the child into this realm:

> Knowledge can be best given when there is eagerness to learn, so this is the period when the seed of everything can be sown, the child's mind being like a fertile field, ready to receive what will germinate into culture. If neglected during this period, or frustrated in its vital needs, the mind of the child becomes artificially dulled, henceforth to resist imparted knowledge. Interest will no longer be there if the seed be sown too late, but at six years of age all items of culture are received enthusiastically, and later these seeds will expand and grow.[23]

Montessori elementary students will not have the distressing struggle of initially confronting the "Who am I?" question in their adolescent or adult years. They will have been comfortable with it since their second phase of development and will be able to use it in ensuing years as a touchstone when making major decisions in their lives. They will have an inner guidance system that seems to be lacking in so many young people in our society today. They will already know something about who they are and what their purpose is in life. What a wonderful benefit to have as they are launched into the real world! Whether or not they have been raised in a religious family,

---

23   Maria Montessori, *To Educate*, p. 4.

they will have a moral compass to help them live meaningful and ethical lives.

Cosmic Education is indeed the way to prepare children for their future.

Chapter 2

Evolution and Cosmic Education

IF COSMIC EDUCATION IS the philosophical foundation of Montessori elementary education, its major theme is evolution—or the emergence of various species of living organisms from their cosmic ancestors through creative change over time. Evolution is the process by which the cosmic story plays itself out on our planet, it is the vehicle for understanding our place in the world, and it is the unifying theme of the Montessori elementary curriculum.

In November of 1997, some of the best scientific and religious minds in the country gathered in Chicago, at the Field Museum of Natural History, for a conference entitled "The Epic of Evolution." The conference, sponsored by the prestigious American Association for the Advancement of Science (AAAS), was billed as a dialogue between science and religion around the issue of evolution. David Kahn, director of the North American Montessori Teachers Association, noting the opportunity presented by the conference, wisely proclaimed NAMTA a collaborator and helped attract Montessori educators to this unique gathering. One of the authors of this book was fortunate to have attended the conference.

For three days, eminent scientists dialogued with equally eminent theologians and religious thinkers on the subject of evolution. The discussion began with the origins of the cosmos itself and proceeded step by step through the evolution of our planet, of life on Earth, and finally of human beings within this context. It was a unique blend of scientific content which mirrored the Montessori cosmic curriculum within the context of a religious discussion seeking to explore the meaning of these great scientific themes.

The consensus of speakers and participants was that evolution provided the intellectual framework for understanding ourselves and our Universe, and that education should be geared toward introducing children and young adults into this context of understanding. The Montessori educators in the audience found themselves agreeing, suddenly realizing that they already had a pedagogy for elementary-age children that relied on just that curriculum.

The concept of evolution permeates Montessori's entire curriculum for elementary-age children. As a scientist, she accepted the theory of evolution as well established, and she used it as the structure for large portions of the curriculum, particularly those related to biology and history. To understand the Montessori curriculum, we need to understand how she incorporated the idea of evolution into her pedagogy.

Biological Evolution

The most common understanding of the term "evolution" is the scientific theory for the formation and development of the various life forms on Earth, or *biogenesis,* a word of Greek origin meaning life-birth. Scientists have come to believe that the diversity of living species on this planet have all come into being through a process of hereditary continuity and change tracing back to primitive and simple organisms that emerged some 3.5 billion years ago. These first forms of life faithfully passed along the genetic information they had gathered. However, the environment caused millions of changes in that hereditary baggage and further unexpected mutations occurred to produce the vast array of living species on Earth, up to and including humans. This is the scientific theory of evolution.

Although others had proposed evolutionary theories before him, Charles Darwin is generally credited with fathering and popularizing the basic outline of the modern theory of evolution. In his book *Origin of the Species,* published in 1858, the British naturalist argued that all existing species of life could trace their ancestry to more primitive and now extinct organisms that lived millions of years ago. The mechanism by which this speciation occurred, in Darwin's analysis, was a process called *natural selection.* He theorized that organisms with characteristics suited to the environment survived, while other organisms with characteristics less useful in that environment died off. Through many generations of offspring, these subtle variations eventually produced new species.

Darwin generally avoided the issue of human ancestry in his first book, although he eventually addressed this controversial portion of his theory in another book, *The Descent of Man,* published in 1871. Darwin's ideas caused a furor among fellow biologists, religious leaders, and the general public. The idea of human beings descending from "lower" life forms was just too controversial for many to accept.

That controversy led to arguments over whether the theory of evolution should be taught in the schools, with the 1925 "monkey trial" conviction of Tennessee teacher John T. Scopes bringing the issue into heated public debate in the United States. The U.S. Supreme Court ruled in 1968 that laws forbidding the teaching of evolution were unconstitutional, and in 1981 federal courts also overturned an Arkansas law that required public schools to teach creationism, based on the biblical account of Genesis, whenever evolution is taught. However, the issue still raises controversy today—there is a continuing tug-of-war in Kansas, for example, where the state school board voted to remove evolution from the science curriculum in 1999, only to have voters toss out the pro-creationism board in 2000 and go back to teaching the evolution, to subsequent pendulum swings on the school board in 2004 and 2006. In 2007, a 70,000-square-foot Creation Museum opened in northern Kentucky to promote young Earth creationism in the mode of a literal reading of the book of Genesis and to refute the arguments of evolution.

Since Darwin published his ideas, other scientists have gathered evidence to support and modify his theories. Paleontologists showed the structural similarities called homologies that exist between extinct species and many of today's plants and animals. Geneticists learned about DNA and mutations, factors which explain both the continuity and change in heredity throughout generations of offspring.[24] Paleoanthropologists gathered evidence on the existence of ancient species of hominids and early humans.

The scientific evidence soon became overwhelming in support of the theory of evolution. While the mechanism proved to be more complicated than Darwin had theorized—including such factors as mutations and genetic drift (random changes)—the basic theory of species evolving into new species became almost universally accepted in the scientific community of Montessori's time.

With her scientific background in medicine, it was inevitable that she would use these ideas in her pedagogy. The materials she developed in history and biology, in particular, relied heavily on an evolutionary framework—from timelines stretching back billions of years to the origins of life, to animal and plant studies arranged in evolutionary sequence. She did not become an advocate for evolution against the opponents of her time. She merely accepted the scientific consensus as a given and applied it to her pedagogy and her educational materials.

The Place of Humans in Biological Evolution

The specific controversy over human evolution did not deter Montessori from developing a curriculum to teach students about the emergence of the human species as part of the evolutionary story. She, like many of the theorists of evolution in her time, viewed humans as the crowning achievement in the process of evolution. An entire segment of her elementary curriculum is dedicated to this theme, as we shall see later in this book.

Montessori does not discuss extensively where she acquired her ideas on evolution, although she does quote one of the leading philosophers of

---

24 An understandable explanation of the impact of these discoveries can be found in *The Secret of Life: Redesigning the Living World,* by Joseph Levine & David Suzuki. A PBS television series covered the same material.

evolution, Henri Bergson, in her own work, using his ideas about the "élan vital" or "vital urge" that carries evolution forward.[25] Bergson (1859–1941) won the 1927 Nobel Prize for literature, and his ideas had great popularity in Europe during the time Montessori was developing her educational method. Bergson even served as a sponsor for a Montessori school for war orphans and refugee children in France after World War I and visited with Montessori when she was honored at the Sorbonne.[26]

Bergson, in his book *Creative Evolution*, does not see humans as the end purpose of evolution so much as one of the vital branches of consciousness that emerged. Only in humans has consciousness been able to truly escape the confines of matter, particularly through the development of brain, language, and society. As for humankind's evolutionary task, Bergson envisions a humanity in which intellect and intuition are fully developed and combined, using the gains of the intellect without losing the power of instinct to carry life forward. For Bergson, this introduces the realm of the spiritual life, out of the reaches of matter's pull.[27]

Another contemporary whose ideas on evolution were similar to Montessori's was French paleontologist Pierre Teilhard de Chardin (1881–1955). He was a Jesuit priest who was inspired in his work by Bergson, but because his ideas were controversial within his own church, most of his writings were not published until after his death—which was after Montessori's death as well.

Teilhard de Chardin, in his book *The Phenomenon of Man*, described humanity as the bearer of the crown of consciousness, which he called the realm of the Noosphere, a Greek-derived word he coined to signify the sphere of the Spirit. For him, the mechanism which carries evolution forward is a growing complexity accompanied by an expanding consciousness. As this dual growth occurs, reality eventually reaches a critical point where it must transform itself into a new level of existence or cease to exist. Such a transformation occurred on Earth when mega-molecules of carbon and other elements became so complex that they moved our planet into the Biosphere, or the realm of living matter. Another radical shift of evolutionary change, raising reality to yet a new level of existence, took place when life forms

25   Maria Montessori, *To Educate*, p. 21.
26   Rita Kramer, *Maria Montessori*, p. 246, 268.
27   Henri Bergson, *Creative Evolution*, p. 284–292.

became so complex that thought and reflective consciousness were born as humans emerged into the Noosphere.[28]

At this point in evolution, the creatures became creators; the divinely guided process of evolution came under the control of a puny species of animals called humans. What the Universe becomes in the future, whether or not evolution carries it to the next stage of integration of the Spirit into what Teilhard de Chardin called the ultimate unity of the Omega Point, depends on the fragile choices and fallible decisions to be made by humankind.[29]

All three of these mid-20th-century thinkers—Bergson, Teilhard de Chardin, and Montessori—shared the vision that evolution was something that had a purpose, that followed a plan, perhaps even a divine plan. For all of them, the human species, *Homo sapiens*, was the culminating achievement of the process of evolution to date on this planet. They also shared the idea that evolution was still incomplete, that there were tasks yet to be accomplished to advance evolution, to bring the unfolding of the Universe to its ultimate destiny.

Montessori sketched her own ideas on the "cosmic task" of humanity in a variety of lectures and books. Among the most important were those produced while she lived in India—books like *To Educate the Human Potential*, first published by Kalakshetra Publications in 1948.

Perhaps she was influenced by the Theosophical Society or Eastern mysticism in developing these ideas, or perhaps she found familiar echoes of her own Roman Catholic background within the spiritual worlds of Buddhism and Hinduism. Whatever the origin of her ideas, she had a finely tuned concept of the moral imperative of the human race, the kind of existence humans, both collectively and individually, must live in order to fulfill their cosmic task.

In *To Educate the Human Potential,* she writes:

> The laws governing the universe can be made interesting and wonderful to the child, more interesting even than things in themselves, and he begins to ask: What am I? What is the task of man in this wonderful universe? Do we merely live here for ourselves or is there something more for us to do? . . .

---

28 Pierre Teilhard de Chardin, *The Phenomenon of Man*, p. 161 ff.

29 Ibid., p. 235 ff.

Truly it is no new idea, for it has been the natural plan wherever there has been education in the real sense of the word ... for children first to be taught the creation of the world and man's place in it, so far as these questions could be answered in the light of religion and philosophy. The answer was ever what it still is, "God has sent you upon the earth to work and do your duty!"[30]

In a lecture Montessori delivered in India in 1946, she spoke, much like Bergson and Teilhard de Chardin, of the cosmic task of humanity as that of taking charge of creation. After describing the cosmic tasks of other living creatures, Montessori asks:

Is humanity the only parasite who lives among useless struggles and immense work merely to keep itself living? Is it possible that only Man spends his brief span of life suffering in this terrestrial world to no purpose? This cannot be so. It is evident that the cosmic theory must include also man among the agents of creation.... Human intelligence has become almost all powerful and today has arrived at a point where it can dominate the energies of the world and penetrate the most intimate secrets of life.

Therefore, instead of being a parasite, he is the one who not only enjoys the environment, but is the most active of the agents who are destined to modify and perfect it. His energy is almost all-powerful and through his endeavors he has so transformed himself as to become able to realize the miracles of a new creation.

If we compare conditions of the earth before his appearance to the earth as we know it today we get an idea of the power of humanity as a cosmic agent. Yet the span of the existence of humanity when compared to the length of the geological epochs shows humanity to be so young as to enable us to say that it is only at the beginning of its cosmic task. This task seems to be unlimited and to lead to supernatural and divine powers. The intelligence and the sentiments of mankind have evolved through its creative cosmic task. What

---

30   Maria Montessori, *To Educate*, p. 10.

we have today is the realization of what was felt by intuition in the religions of thousands of years ago.³¹

So, for Montessori, like Bergson and Teilhard de Chardin, there is a direction to evolution which leads inexorably to the emergence of humankind, and the human species is the recipient of a cosmic task reflecting that of the divine creator.

Cosmic Evolution

Scientists today tend to think of "evolution" as something which goes well beyond the origin of humans or the birth of life itself on this planet. There is a sense in which evolution can be understood not only as *biogenesis*, but more broadly as *cosmogenesis*, or the evolutionary birth and unfolding of the Universe and all its parts.

That was certainly the sense of the word adopted by the scientists and theologians who gathered in Chicago in 1997. The conference was entitled "The Epic of Evolution," and it traced the story of evolution from the birth of the Universe in the Big Bang, through the birth of the stars and planets, to life on Earth and the emergence of humans, and eventually through yet another meaning of evolution as the cultural changes studied by anthropologists and historians. Evolution, an epic story, encompasses all of those 15 billion years of birth and change!

Two of the speakers at that conference, mathematical cosmologist Brian Swimme and cultural anthropologist Thomas Berry, collaborated on a book called *The Universe Story,* which summarizes that epic story in language that can be understood by the layman. In fact, the book could serve as a blueprint for Montessori teachers wanting to flesh out with modern scholarship the outline of Cosmic Education developed by Maria Montessori for her elementary curriculum.³²

This view of the history of the Universe as an evolving reality is one that is taught in university settings today under the rubric of "Big History."

---

31 Maria Montessori (1989),"Cosmic Education" in *The Child, Society and the World: Unpublished Speeches and Writings*. Oxford, England: Clio Press, p. 106 ff.

32 Brian Swimme and Thomas Berry, *The Universe Story: from the Primordial Flaring Forth to the Ecozoic Era—a Celebration of the Unfolding of the Cosmos.*

David Christian, a professor at San Diego State University and one of the main proponents of this view of history, offers a course that mirrors that of Cosmic Education in many ways.

In a course book accompanying his 48-lecture series for The Teaching Company, he writes, "Big history surveys the past at all possible scales, from conventional history, to the much larger scales of biology and geology, to the universal scales of cosmology. It weaves a single story, stretching from the origins of the Universe to the present day and beyond, using accounts of the past developed within scholarly disciplines that are usually studied quite separately."[33]

Montessori, who died in 1952, nevertheless had a vision of evolution that included the Universe in a surprisingly modern way. She was not content to tell children just the story of life and the first humans. She wanted to give them an understanding of the Universe itself. She wanted to place their understanding of themselves—"Where do I come from?"—in the context of the entire cosmos, not merely within the parochial view of the planet Earth. She wanted to address the question of "Why am I here?" with the understanding that the "here" is the Universe, not just this planet. She believed that human beings were the offspring of the Universe and that they—like all other creatures—had a cosmic task.

Montessori saw no contradiction between her acceptance of evolution and her religious beliefs as a Roman Catholic. In fact, much like Teilhard de Chardin, she considered human beings as collaborators with the deity in the work of continuing creation. In this view, the biblical account of creation is not to be taken literally, but rather is a story designed to establish a religious truth—that humans are ultimately dependent for their existence on a Creator.[34] Seeing humans in the context of Cosmic Evolution helps identify their most fundamental moral imperative, their cosmic task.

The ideas expressed by Montessori and Teilhard de Chardin hold less appeal in the more secular world we live in today. Indeed, many in

---

33   The title of Professor David Christian's course is Big History: The Big Bang, Life on Earth, and the Rise of Humanity, providing a direct parallel to the three Great Lessons in Montessori called the Creation Story, the Story of Life, and the Story of Humans (to be discussed later in this book). The 2008 DVD course is available through The Teaching Company in Chantilly, VA. Christian has also written a book on the subject called *Maps of Time: An Introduction to Big History*. University of California Press, Berkeley, CA 2004.

34   A more detailed discussion of the religious controversy over the theory of evolution can be found in a postscript at the end of this chapter.

the scientific world would deny any plan or purpose to evolution itself, preferring to see the evolution of the human species as a random event in the midst of millions of other random events in the history of the Universe.

Indeed, our ability today to look beyond our own planet Earth through the miracle of space exploration radically changes our perspective and makes it difficult to imagine humans having such an exalted task as continuing the process of divine creation. It's one thing to *know*, as thinkers as far back as the Babylonians and Aristotle knew, that there is a vast Universe out there beyond our planet and our human existence. It is quite another to *appreciate* that reality by stepping gingerly off our own planetary rock into the vastness of space or looking out into the immense distances of the Universe with such instruments as the Hubble telescope.

With modern secularity and this new perspective on the Universe, some scientists are reluctant to see intentionality in the process of evolution, to attribute its outcomes to any sort of plan. Stephen Jay Gould, who popularized the study of natural history for many in this generation, consistently maintains that the sweep of evolutionary history is "partly random and, in any case, not designed for us or toward us."[35] For him, our past is contingent, not inevitable and predictable. We are an accident of history, one out of many possible products of the evolutionary process.

It is even more inconceivable to a scientist like Gould that humans have any special role to play in evolutionary history. He speaks derisively of the arrogance or "hubris" of humans to conclude that they can affect the planet we live on in any significant fashion or, worse, to consider themselves "stewards" who must save the planet. The most that Gould will concede is that we have a legitimate "parochial concern for our own species and the current planetary configurations that now support us."[36]

Not every scientist of today agrees with Gould. Many would see an undeniable purpose or at least direction to evolution. Certainly, many of the scientists and religious thinkers who gathered in Chicago in 1997 saw a more active role for humans on this planet than the mere preservation of our own species and all that is required to keep it alive. Many would agree with Montessori that we humans have a "cosmic task," or at least a planetary task.

---

35 Stephen Jay Gould, *The Flamingo's Smile: Reflections in Natural History*, p. 15.
36 Stephen Jay Gould, *Bully for Brontosaurus: Reflections in Natural History*, p. 17.

It is certainly not within the scope of this book to settle the question of the meaning of life in this new context, to decide whether divine wisdom or sheer random chance guides the Universe. Each of us must ponder that question for himself or herself. However we deal with that question, Montessori's ideas on Cosmic Education retain a validity in the classroom as we guide children in developing a sense of their place in the Universe.

Those scientists and religious thinkers who gathered in Chicago to discuss the Epic of Evolution recognized humans as the chief protagonists in this heroic story, whatever the origin of their species. On the final day of the conference, they also talked extensively about the obligations imposed on humans by their privileged position of consciousness in guiding the future course of evolution on our planet. Because of the undeniable impact of our own species on the life of the planet, we have a moral responsibility—a "cosmic task"—to deal with such problems as global warming, pollution controls, management of natural resources, population growth, the impact of industrial development, protection of endangered species, a responsible use of biotechnology, and other global concerns.

Our ability to affect our own planet is undisputed. Indeed we are more aware of it today than in Montessori's own time. For all practical purposes, whether our task is cosmic, global or, to reduce it to Gould's level, merely species-specific, there is a vision we must impart to our children, there is a need to make them aware of their place in the Universe, and there is a mandate for carrying out the Cosmic Education suggested by Montessori.

The survival of our species almost certainly depends on it. The welfare of our planet probably hangs in the balance. Perhaps, in some way we don't yet understand, we affect the Universe as well.

POSTSCRIPT

A word must be added here about what Montessori teachers can say to those who have religious beliefs which conflict with the teaching of evolution. If the thesis of this chapter is correct, a Montessori school must teach evolution to remain true to the vision of Cosmic Education. Teaching math and language in a Montessori style without including lessons on biology and history structured around the framework of evolution would not be faithful to Montessori's views of Cosmic Education; teaching evolution quietly, without letting parents really know the extent of the evolutionary pattern in the elementary curriculum, would be deceptive and dishonest. So, how do we talk to concerned parents? We have to understand parents' belief systems before we can adequately answer their questions.

If parents are neutral to evolution from a religious perspective and are concerned only about the science, we should be prepared to tell them simply that we teach evolution as the most widely accepted theory of the way the Universe, life, and humans have come to be. The National Science Teachers Association produced a position statement in 1997 that summarizes the rationale for teaching evolution, stating that the NSTA "supports the position that evolution is a major unifying concept of science and should be included as part of K–College frameworks and curricula."[37] While acknowledging a history of public misunderstanding, politics, controversy, and even intimidation of teachers over the issue, the NSTA states that "there is abundant and consistent evidence from astronomy, physics, biochemistry, geochronology, geology, biology, anthropology and other sciences that evolution has taken place."

As a scientific theory, the NSTA states, evolution has been shown to be internally consistent with the available evidence, firmly grounded on that evidence, and tested against a wide range of phenomena. "There is no longer a debate among scientists over whether evolution has taken place. There is considerable debate about how evolution has taken place: the processes and mechanisms producing change, and what has happened during the history of the universe." While any scientific theory is subject to change as more evidence is uncovered, evolution remains the most consistent and acceptable explanation for "the idea that the universe has a history: that change through time has taken place."

Montessori teachers and administrators may need to say more than this to parents who approach the question from a religious perspective, particularly in light of the Creation Story accepted by the dominant monotheistic religions in our society—Judaism, Christianity, and Islam. The Genesis

---

[37] The National Science Teachers Association board of directors adopted the position statement on evolution in July, 1997. The full text of the statement is available at www.nsta.org.

account of God creating the Universe, life, and humans in seven days does not seem to be compatible with the theory of evolution.

Once again, we must know the beliefs of our parents before we can address their concerns. Do they believe the sacred texts are to be taken literally, with all the details accepted as historically and scientifically accurate? Or do they accept a less literal interpretation of the Creation Story that stresses the religious nature of the message and leaves room for different historical details?

For some branches of Judaism, Christianity, and Islam, there is no contradiction between faith and science, between purely religious beliefs about a creative God and the scientific theory of evolution. For theologians and religious leaders in these traditions, the Creation Story of Genesis expresses a religious truth that God is the Creator of all that is and the foundation of everything in the Universe, that everything in the cosmos exists because of God's gift of self in the act of Creation. The story in which this religious truth is embedded, the historical and scientific details of how this occurred, is not what is important. Faith addresses itself to the belief that God is Creator—however God chose to exercise that power in the Universe.

For these believers, the scientific theory of evolution does not go far enough to explain the origins of the Universe. Even scientists stumble when they try to explain what produced the Big Bang to begin with, what set the whole process of evolution in motion. A God who creates is one possible explanation for those who choose to believe in the religious truth expressed in the book of Genesis. In fact, for such believers, the simple and poetic account of the creation stories[38] is enriched and complemented by the scientific account of cosmic and biological evolution in such a way that even more awe is generated in the believer. There is an even greater appreciation for the creative power of God in the context of the details of evolution—e.g., the delicate balance of forces that keep the Universe from either collapsing into nothingness or expanding into unconnected particles scattered across infinite space, the incredible mixture of elements and energy that makes the Earth a life-producing planet, or the millions of genetic transformations that eventually produced the human species.

---

38 For biblical scholars in this tradition, there are actually two separate creation accounts in Genesis, one from the Yahwistic tradition in Chapter 1 and another from the Eloistic tradition in Chapter 2.

More moderate believers in these religious traditions also accept the theory of evolution as something that can enhance faith rather than destroy it. The Roman Catholic Church, which has a long history of resisting scientific advances from Copernicus to Galileo, has come to terms with the theory of evolution in our time. Pope John Paul II addressed the Pontifical Academy of Sciences in 1996 on the subject of evolution and reminded the members that "truth cannot contradict truth." He noted that Pope Pius XII, in a 1950 encyclical, "had already stated that there was no opposition between evolution and the doctrine of the faith about man and his vocation," as long as the evolution of the human body does not leave God out of the creation of the human soul. John Paul continues: "Today, almost half a century after publication of the encyclical, new knowledge has led to the recognition of the theory of evolution as something more than a hypothesis," with a convergence of evidence from various fields of knowledge producing "a significant argument in favor of this theory."[39]

A particularly good resource for helping Christian believers deal with the seeming difficulties of accepting evolution is the book *Thank God for Evolution: How the Marriage of Science and Religion Will Transform Your Life and World*, by Michael Dowd (Plume 2009). Dowd was pastor of United Church of Christ congregations before becoming an "evolutionary evangelist," traveling around the country with his wife, science writer Connie Barlow, over most of the past decade to share their enthusiasm for this story.

For parents from fundamentalist traditions, be they Jews, Christians, or Muslims, the issue is a lot more difficult. They believe in the Creation Story of Genesis as a literal account of how the world and humans came to be. This is in direct conflict with the theory of evolution. We, as teachers, have no right to contradict or challenge the religious beliefs they choose to pass on to their children.

Even here, however, there is room for accommodation. As good scientists, we should stress that evolution is a theory, however well-founded it may seem to be, and that every scientific theory is subject to change as new evidence is gathered. If these parents can live with the presentation of evolution as a theory, leaving their child the choice to reject it in favor of religious beliefs, this may be enough to defuse the situation. A further argument can be made to these parents that, even if they reject evolution for religious rea-

---

[39] Pope John Paul II, Message to Pontifical Academy of Sciences, October 22, 1996.

sons, their children should at least be aware of what the dominant scientific theory of their culture is if they want to be fully educated members of that society. As long as they can trust the teacher not to impose that theory on their children as gospel, perhaps they can see the value of their children learning about evolution—and remaining free to reject it.

If parents remain uncomfortable with their children being exposed to the theory of evolution, despite the arguments above, we should be honest enough to say to them that we can't teach Montessori's Cosmic Education and isolate their child from exposure to evolution. It's not like a sex education class that they can choose to join or skip—the theory permeates the entire cultural curriculum. For these children, it is better that they go elsewhere for their education, out of respect for their family's religious beliefs and to avoid a dichotomy within the child between what they are being taught at home and at school.

Montessori schools must always respect the belief systems of their students, but they must also remain up front and honest about the teaching of evolution and Cosmic Education if they are to call themselves Montessori schools.

Chapter 3

Cosmic Education and the Cultural Curriculum

I F COSMIC EDUCATION IS the underlying philosophy and evolution the primary theme of the Montessori elementary program, the subjects which together comprise what we call the "cultural curriculum" are its core. These subjects, which have to do with passing on to later generations the accumulated wisdom of past "cultures," are the primary emphasis of education at the elementary level for Montessori. An integrated curriculum of history, geography, biology, and physical sciences is the heart and soul of an authentic Montessori elementary classroom.

In traditional schools, math and language are the primary focus of the early elementary years, and those two disciplines certainly have a major place in Montessori classrooms. In Cosmic Education, children learn through the history of language and math how important these two gifts are and how we should be grateful to the inventors of each. Language and math are the tools children use to explore their cultural heritage.

In fact, Montessori has developed brilliant, hands-on materials for teaching these two subjects in a most effective way. The bead frames, checkerboard, and racks and tubes are examples of these materials for teaching the basic operations of arithmetic. Like all Montessori math materials, they stress understanding over memorization, process over product, problem-solving over merely getting the right answer. In upper elementary, there are the advanced fraction materials, the decimal checkerboard, and materials like the trinomial cube to teach such concepts as cube roots in a concrete, visual way that leads to true understanding of the process.

In language, there are phonograms, grammar boxes, and sentence analysis materials to teach reading, parts of speech, and Montessori-style diagraming. Once again, the concrete, visual nature of the materials lends itself to real understanding rather than memorization, to self-directed learning rather than passive reception of knowledge about the processes of reading and writing.

These are definite strengths of a Montessori classroom. However, if math and language dominate the classroom, if they take up the majority of the time of students and teachers, something is out of sync and it is not a faithful following of Montessori's ideas about educating young people in the second plane of development.

For a truly integrated curriculum centered around the cultural subjects, math and language should be called upon to serve that cultural core. Literature selections can complement the cultural subjects being studied, and writing can be focused around children's research reports or attempts at historical fiction based on the cultural subjects. Math also can be useful in the production of historical timelines that demonstrate the relative proportions of the different eras.

Everything in an authentic Montessori classroom revolves around the cultural curriculum, that mixture of history and science, story and study.

The Great Lessons of the Montessori Curriculum

In the classic Montessori elementary program, there are five "great stories" or "great lessons" around which much of the rest of the curriculum is arranged. These are the Creation Story or Story of the Universe; the Story of Life; the Story of Humans; the Story of Math; and the Story of Language.[40]

---

40 Grazzini, p. 43. Grazzini listed a sixth great lesson, the Story of the Great River, or human biology, although this is not one of the five listed in the usual Montessori canon.

The first three are the main chapters in the all-encompassing "Epic of Evolution," which tells the story of our origin and our past, while the last two are illustrations of human cultural accomplishments and the evolution of human ideas.

Maria Montessori herself apparently did not identify these five lessons as a special selection of stories, although she did talk about the elements of all these stories and many others in *To Educate the Human Potential*, which is a conceptual guide for the entire elementary curriculum. Elsewhere, she focuses on three areas of study as particularly important preparations for adult life: 1) the study of the Earth and of living things (the Story of Life), 2) the study of the history of humanity (the Story of Humans), and 3) the study of human progress and the building up of civilizations (the Story of Civilizations).[41]

According to Camillo Grazzini, it was Mario Montessori who developed the concept of the "cosmic fables" in a series of workshops in Perugia, Italy, in the summer of 1956, four years after his mother's death. Grazzini, who attended these workshops along with other practicing Montessori educators, said Mario Montessori at times referred to these five as "great lessons," emphasizing the content, and at other times as "great stories," emphasizing the form of presentation.[42] It was at these workshops that materials were developed to illustrate the Great Lessons.

In a December 2000 online discussion of the Great Lessons stimulated by a question on several Montessori list-serves, Montessori educators from diverse backgrounds came up with a variety of explanations for the emphasis on these lessons, including several who cited the work of Margaret Stephenson, one of the pioneer trainers in this country. David Kahn reports that, in a conversation with Grazzini, he was told the Story of the Universe (Creation Story/God Who Has No Hands) was created by Mario Montessori after he discussed it with his mother; the Story of Life and the Story of Humans were written by Mario Montessori; and the Story of Language and the Story of Math were developed by followers of Montessori, including Grazzini and Stephenson.

It is quite evident from these discussions that there is nothing sacred about the number five—Grazzini himself listed six. What is important is

---

41 Maria Montessori, *From Childhood*, p. 76–79.

42 Grazzini, p. 42.

the role these lessons play in the Montessori curriculum. They are special lessons because the content of the entire Montessori curriculum can be organized around them and because they are the pedagogical format used to inspire the study of the students. They are what Montessori educators call "impressionistic lessons," designed to introduce an overview of content while inspiring students to further study.

Following the organizational guide of the Epic of Evolution, we suggest that there are other chapters in the evolutionary story that could be introduced to fill in the narrative between the Creation Story/Story of the Universe and the Story of Life. This is just another way to synthesize the broad scope of the Montessori elementary curriculum, using a mental organization that pulls all the parts together into a coherent whole.

David Christian, mentioned in the previous chapter, recognizes the benefit of creating a unified discipline of Big History. In his more sophisticated version of Cosmic Education, there are eight chapters—or thresholds of developing complexity: the creation of the Universe, stars, chemical elements, planets and Earth, life on Earth, our species, agriculture, and the modern revolution.

"Human history is seen as part of the history of our Earth and biosphere, and the Earth's history, in turn, is seen as part of the history of the Universe. In this way, the different disciplines that make up this large story can be used to illuminate each other. The unified account of the past assembled in this way can help us understand our own place within the Universe," he writes, using an imagery that matches the concept behind the cover of this book and the principal themes of Montessori's Great Lessons.

That unifying story, after all, is what Maria Montessori was trying to teach us. These stories, and other impressionistic lessons like them, are the linchpins of the whole curriculum, providing the big picture for the studies done in the elementary program. They are the glue that holds it all together. Story comes first—then study.

In discussing the Great Lessons, Paula Polk Lillard explains the rationale behind presenting children with the big picture as the context for their study: "Giving the children the universe as a context for their further study solves the problem of the children's accumulation of isolated bits and pieces of knowledge with no way of relating one to another. The children's power of reason is stimulated to search for the connections between all things."[43]

Maria Montessori herself, in *To Educate the Human Potential*, explains it in her own more florid style: "Interest spreads to all, for all are linked and have their place in the universe in which the mind is centered. The stars, earth, stones, life of all kinds form a whole in relation with each other, and so close is this relation that we cannot understand a stone without some understanding of the great sun."[44]

In other words, in the view of Montessori herself and others, it is pointless to argue over how many great lessons there should be. There is only *one* story, the comprehensive story of the changing Universe itself, and the division into separate lessons is just the way we humans must proceed to make it accessible and understandable.

The story takes on many names, depending on who's telling it. In addition to being called Cosmic Education (Montessori) or Big History (David Christian), it is also known as The Universe Story (Brian Swimme/Thomas Berry), The Epic of Evolution (American Association for the Advancement of Science), Deep Time (David Darling), or the New Creation Story (various religious figures). The confluence of all these thinkers and storytellers has led Jennifer Morgan, author of a trilogy for children on the subject, to attempt to put together a website linking all of these sources.

The story that all of these movements hope to impart is one that basically explores the origins of everything, with each origin story embedded in yet another—the organizational schema for understanding that is represented graphically on the cover of this book.

What we would hope for as an outcome to the Cosmic Education curriculum at the elementary level would be students who emerge with a basic grasp of the broad outlines of this story, from Big Bang to our modern society. This general knowledge is more important than the individual scientific concepts contained along the way in the different chapters of the story.

Hopefully, this would not be the only exposure students get to the comprehensive story of Big History/Cosmic Education in the course of their formal education. Learning about the universal story should be something experienced in a spiral, with deeper understanding of its implications for

---

43 Lillard, *Montessori Today*, p. 55–56.

44 Maria Montessori, *To Educate*, p. 9.

our lives at each level of education.

While Cosmic Education was developed specifically with the elementary student (ages 6–12) in mind, the Montessori primary level (ages 3–6) should—as with every aspect of the curriculum—sow the seeds and lay the foundation for later learning.

Two resources that 3–6 teachers should be familiar with are: the book *I Wonder What's Out There*, by Joanne Alex, which provides age-appropriate activities for 3–6 students related to Cosmic Education; the other resource is the "Cosmic Wonder" series by Aline Wolf, a simple and accessible set of booklets with the titles:

- *I Live in the Universe*
- *I Look "Out" at the Stars*
- *I Travel on Planet Earth*
- *I Know What Gravity Does*
- *How Big is the Milky Way?*
- *I Know the Sun Does Not "Set"*[45]

On the other side of the elementary spectrum, Montessori middle and high school students should continue the study of Cosmic Education as an important element of their curriculum. Students at these levels can gain a much deeper understanding of the various scientific concepts involved in each chapter of the story; adolescents are especially attuned to the task of exploring their identity (Who am I?) in a widening context; and this age group has an emerging sense of taking responsibility for the implications of Cosmic Education in real life situations—conflict resolution, social justice, environmental awareness, and the search for the ultimate meaning of everything.

The International Big History Association (IBHA), in its first conference in August of 2012, highlighted several projects that could be invaluable resources for Montessori middle and high school teachers as they attempt to incorporate Cosmic Education into their curriculum. We wrote an article for *Montessori Life* in 2013 about our participation in that conference that provides details about the intersection of Big History and Montessori's Cosmic Education.

One valuable resource we found is ChronoZoom (chronozoom.com), an

---

[45] All of these books are available through Montessori Services, which in 2013 purchased the original publishing company, Parent Child Press.

open source project being developed jointly by Microsoft and the University of California at Berkeley. According to its developers, "ChronoZoom is an intuitive online tool used to visualize all of time, from the Big Bang to today, using the concept of zooming along the timeline to express distance to highlight the scope of time. . . . You can browse through history on ChronoZoom to find data in the form of articles, images, video, sound, and other multimedia."

Given the prominent place of timelines in Montessori education, this resource provides an interactive, technologically contemporary, scientifically updated tool to explore the entire scope of the Universe Story, not only for junior high and high school students, but for Montessori upper elementary students as well.

Another IBHA resource is The Big History Project, a Bill Gates-funded attempt to translate the Big History narrative into a high school curriculum. This too is a free, open source, online course (bighistoryproject.com) that covers the entire scope of Big History/Cosmic Education. Piloted in recent years in a limited number of schools, it is being finalized in 2013 for more widespread use—and will be available to anyone who wants to use it in their classrooms.

The solidity of the science, the slick presentation of the content, and the commitment to telling the comprehensive story could serve the growing number of Montessori schools around the country opening middle school classes, as well as the more limited number of high schools. Given our elementary students' familiarity with Cosmic Education, it would even be accessible for our upper elementary students—and serve as an invaluable resource of information and pedagogical ideas for our teachers.

The content of these resources is not a dry, textbook-style presentation of information. Like our own approach to Cosmic Education, it is based on the idea of telling a story, fleshing out the narrative one chapter at a time.

In addition to providing the conceptual center for unifying knowledge, a story approach also gives the learner the emotional tie that makes the knowledge meaningful and worth remembering. Again, in the words of Montessori, "If the idea of the universe be presented to the child in the right way, it will do more for him than just arouse his interest, for it will create in him admiration and wonder, a feeling loftier than any interest and more satisfying."[46]

Montessori's words are validated by the conclusions of modern educational psychologists who insist on the emotional component of learning. Models of information processing stress the importance of the input of emotions on motivation and long-term memory.[47] Brain research demonstrates the intimate interconnections between frontal cortex and limbic regions of the brain, between the thinking parts and the centers of emotion in the brain.[48] Modern science has come to conclusions that support Montessori's approach of appealing to the emotions to make learning more effective.

This is the approach of Montessori's "impressionistic" lessons, which are stories with the power to fire the child's imagination and stimulate interest in further study—however many of them we choose to include in our classrooms. Although there are five privileged stories in the classic Montessori canon, there are many other equally impressive stories (sometimes called "key lessons") embedded within those core stories. However, there are opportunities for Montessori teachers with a creative streak and storytelling skills to expand the repertoire of stories even further, based on current scientific thought.

Story and Study

Story and study are the two main components of the Montessori cultural curriculum. Storytelling comes first—then comes the detailed study.

A successful Montessori teacher is a good storyteller. Without having to become a professional storyteller, it is important for the teacher to develop a facility for telling simple stories with drama and some flair to hook the students' interest in a subject or area of study. Only in this way can the riches of the cultural studies be opened to the imagination and interest of the child. The impressionistic presentations of the Great Lessons and other subsidiary presentations in the transmission of human culture are critical components in the repertoire of the Montessori teacher or "directress."

---

46 Maria Montessori, *To Educate*, pp. 9, 32.
47 R. H. Bruning, G. J. Schraw, and R. R. Ronning, *Cognitive Psychology and Instruction*, p. 8–9.
48 D. Goleman, *Emotional Intelligence*, p. 9–12.

The job of the Montessori teacher/directress is not to *teach* information so much as to *guide or direct* the children into an area of study by stimulating their imagination and interest, and then letting them go on their own as far as they wish using both the classroom materials and outside resources.

The story part is the principal job of the teacher; the study part is primarily the job of the students, although some presentations involve an introduction of information by the teacher as well. Once the impressionistic lessons have been given, the children are ready to pursue a subject as far as their interest will carry them. There are well-developed classroom materials in most areas to further guide their study, as will be explained in later chapters of this book, and all the teacher needs to do is show the students how to use the materials—not teach all the information contained in them. If the teacher falls into the temptation of dispensing all the information so that she is sure the students get it, two things will happen: 1) the students will fall into the passive mode of memorize and regurgitate, so prevalent in traditional education; and 2) their "study" will be circumscribed by the limits imposed by the teacher's own research and knowledge of a field, in many instances depriving them of the opportunity to carry their study far beyond the teacher's own knowledge. Both results inhibit the excitement and satisfaction that are part of an authentic Montessori classroom.

Montessori teachers must confine themselves to the big picture and resist the temptation to share all the details of their knowledge. They provide the main outlines in the impressionistic lessons through stories that inspire the children to further study. They must also remember that the elementary curriculum is a six-year program, and not everything can be covered at one time or within a single year.[49]

History in Cosmic Education

One of the main areas of the Montessori curriculum where Cosmic Education is at work is in the whole strand of presentations involving history. It is here that we find the main stories that the Montessori teacher should master. This is the core component in an integrated cultural curriculum.

---

49 A fuller discussion of the six-year scope and sequence of the Montessori elementary cultural curriculum can be found in the Appendices at the back of this book.

Although history looks primarily at the past, it provides the indispensable context for understanding the present and planning the future, or discovering the cosmic task of humans. Without an understanding of who we are and how we got here, it is impossible to understand what our task in the Universe is.

Carl Sagan and Ann Druyan, in their book *Shadows of Forgotten Ancestors*, write from the perspective of contemporary scientific thought about the random nature of the human phenomenon, but their introduction of the question they address in this 1992 publication sounds very similar to Maria Montessori during her days in India:

"Who are we?" they ask. "Where do we come from? Why are we this way and not some other? What does it mean to be human? Are we capable, if need be, of fundamental change, or do the dead hands of forgotten ancestors impel us in some direction, indiscriminately for good or ill, and beyond our control? . . . In the long run, are we wise enough to know what changes to make? Can we be trusted with our own future?"

They go on to speak of the difficulty of reconstructing a past that stretches back hundreds of thousands of years, or even millions of years if we consider our primate ancestors and the first mammals, or billions of years if we go back to the origins of life itself.

"Our written records carry us only a millionth of the way back to the origin of life. Our beginnings, the key events of our early development, are not readily accessible to us. . . . We humans are like a newborn baby left on a doorstep, with no note explaining who it is, where it came from, what hereditary cargo of attributes and disabilities it might be carrying, or who its antecedents might be. We long to see the orphan's file."[50]

It is this "longing to see the orphan's file" which is at the heart of the Montessori history curriculum. We can only understand our cosmic task if we explore how we got here, where we come from, who we are—we can only discover and accept our cosmic task if we search for our own history, the story of our past, the tale of our ancestry.

There are two elements involved in such a study of history—the telling of the story is one; the other is the marking of time with some sort of clock. Maria Montessori recognized both of these elements in the development of her cultural curriculum.

---

50 Carl Sagan and Ann Druyan, *Shadows of Forgotten Ancestors: A Search for Who We Are*, p. 4–5.

She centers her history curriculum around the telling of stories—the Story of the Universe, the Story of Life, and the Story of Humans. In her cosmic approach to education, each story is a nesting doll placed within the context of a more universal setting, a concentric circle narrowing in toward the child. To complete the entire Epic of Evolution, we suggest the development of a Story of the Solar System and a Story of the Earth to flesh out the narrative between the first two Great Lessons—the Creation Story and the Story of Life—drawing on Montessori's own materials in those areas and the insights of modern science. Then, there are nesting circles of stories to be developed within the third Great Lesson—the Story of Human Civilizations, to which Montessori devoted a lot of attention; the story of a particular nation in the human family, such as American History; and, ultimately, the story of an individual child in its nuclear family.

Each child, each human being, has an important personal story that contributes to the history of its nation; each nation's story is part of the broader history of the human race; the story of the human race is just a chapter in the history of life on Earth; the story of life is only a small part of the bigger story of the Earth itself; the Earth is just the third planet from the Sun, part of a solar system that has its own story; and our solar system is an almost insignificant dot in the vast expanse of galaxies which form the Universe.

The driving force that moves us from one scale in time and space to the next, according to Christian, is the development of increasing complexity. He defines complexity as the binding of diverse components into larger structures which display "emergent properties" not present in their components and which allow the new entity to possess a certain stability. Energy flows are necessary to bind simple components into complex structures, and each threshold involves greater flows of energy—from particles, to stars, to advanced elements, to planets, to life, to humans, to modern societies.

It is the Story of the Universe itself which provides the context for all the rest. This is Cosmic Education, and it centers around storytelling. Maria Montessori, Mario Montessori, and Montessori educators who have come after them have developed a repertoire of stories in which we can situate our own personal histories. These stories can be used as handed down in the Montessori tradition or elaborated on and modernized through the insights of contemporary science. Montessori's Great Lessons are a model and challenge to those who follow her, not a dogmatic recipe book for the whole curriculum.

Montessori did not neglect the other element of history, the element of time and the establishment of a clock to measure the passage of time. Timelines are a fixture in every Montessori classroom in the world, with the earliest classical Montessori timeline starting with the story of the Earth itself and measured by the Clock of Eons. We stretch the latter portion of that timeline into the Timeline of Life. Then, we extend the final strip of that timeline into the Timeline of Humans, the story of our species on this Earth. Many Montessori classrooms extend these timelines backward to the beginnings of the Universe itself and forward into the history of civilizations, our individual nations and even to the level of the individual children in our classes. Once again, it is the universal scope of these timelines that we call Cosmic Education.

Conclusion

This cosmic dimension of the study of history is one of the most important differences between Montessori classrooms and traditional education. Social studies in the traditional classroom go from family, to community, state, nation, and world—the opposite direction from Montessori classrooms. The study of history, in particular, in traditional elementary schools focuses on the fairly parochial story of a nation or, at best, a hemisphere of our tiny planet. Children memorize dates related to events in the story of Western civilization, with kings and presidents and other rulers making up the characters of the story, and wars and trade and advances in technology providing the plot of the story. The story can be an interesting one, but the perspective is paltry without placing it in a larger context of understanding.

This is what Montessori has done with her ideas about Cosmic Education. She breaks the barriers of nations and Western civilization to tell about the human race; she goes beyond the parochial limits of the human story to that of life itself. The history of life is just a small part of a much bigger story, which she called "the cosmic evolution of the universe."[51] As in all Montessori cultural studies, she uses the whole to better understand the parts.

An understanding of this cosmic perspective is essential if we are to be true to Montessori's vision of education. In the next section of this book we take a closer look at the way the human story fits into the much larger story of the cosmos itself, to examine the Montessori history curriculum as part of Cosmic Education.

This will not provide Montessori teachers any new *techniques* for teaching history, nor will it provide any essentially new *content* for the history curriculum. It is merely intended to remind us of the *vision* that must integrate all the individual elements of the cultural curriculum, the Montessori conception of what it is to teach children through Cosmic Education.

---

51 Maria Montessori, "What is Cosmic Education?" From a handwritten manuscript dated October 1949 and included in the publication edited by Grazia Honegger Fresco, *Montessori: perche no? Una pedagogia per la crescita*. FrancoAngeli, Milan, Italy, 2000, p. 167.

Chapter 4

The Story of the Universe

WHEN SHE EXAMINED HISTORY, Maria Montessori's starting point was the history of the Universe itself. Each part of the story after that was like a concentric circle which must be seen within the context of the first, all-containing circle of the cosmos. The Story of the Universe, the fundamental origin story, was the ultimate context in which she sought to place the children's learning. It was a kind of philosophical background for everything else they would learn. "To interest the children in the universe, we must not begin by giving them elementary facts about it, to make them merely understand its mechanism, but start with far loftier notions of a philosophical nature, put in an acceptable manner, suited to the child's psychology."[52]

Brian Swimme and Thomas Berry, in their book *The Universe Story*, complain that "in the modern period, we are without a comprehensive story of the universe. The historians, even when articulating world history, deal not with the whole world but just with humans, as if humans were something separate from or an addendum to the story of the Earth and the universe."[53] Maria Montessori did not make that mistake. Her Cosmic

---

52 Maria Montessori, *To Educate*, p. 28.

53 Swimme and Berry, *The Universe Story*, p. 1.

Education places the entire curriculum of history and other cultural studies within the context of the whole, the Universe.[54]

The Creation Story

The Story of the Universe can be told with a creative God as the main character of the story; it can be told in terms of modern scientific theories of the Big Bang and an expanding, evolving, growing Universe; or the two approaches can be combined into one. Mario Montessori brought the two points of view together in his version of the Creation Story, one of the so-called "great lessons" taught to the youngest of our elementary-age children. (Montessori schools typically divide the elementary program into lower elementary, for 6–9-year-olds, and upper, for 9–12-year-olds.)

This story is called a Great Lesson because so many parts of our curriculum can be grounded in this simple, yet profound story. It is the first lesson in our children's studies of chemistry and physics, their first introduction to astronomy, the first step in the evolutionary story of the biology of life and the human species, the first moment in the history of the cosmos, the first moment in the geology of our planet, and the first in the national and personal history of all of us as humans.

Because of the importance of this seminal story for the whole Montessori curriculum and for Cosmic Education, we want to examine it in detail as a model of the impressionistic story followed by detailed study. The following are excerpts from Mario Montessori's "God Who Has No Hands" story:[55]

From the very beginning, people have been aware of the Great Spirit.[56]

---

54 In these chapters, curriculum descriptions are based on presentations at the Center for Montessori Teacher Education in New York, where both of us received our elementary training. These trace their origins to the AMI center in Bergamo, Italy, where some CMTE/NY trainers acquired their own Montessori formation. That Bergamo curriculum was itself developed by Mario Montessori with the guidance of Maria Montessori in such works as *To Educate the Human Potential*. There have been modifications over the years. However, all Montessori teachers, whatever their training, background, or affiliation, would recognize similar versions of these presentations as part of the traditional repertoire in their classrooms.

55 Quoted from the CMTE/NY history album, with some modifications to change gender references.

56 Mario Montessori used the word "God" in his version of the Creation Story, but we have substituted "Great Spirit" throughout the text to avoid the assignment of a male gender to a genderless deity, to escape the cultural anthropomorphism associated with "God," and to enhance the universal appeal of the story for all the peoples of the Earth, regardless of religious background or beliefs.

> *They could feel the Spirit, though they could not see it. . . . It has no eyes to see with, no hands to work with, and no feet to walk with; but it sees everything and knows everything. . . .*
>
> *In the beginning there was only the Great Spirit. Since the Spirit was completely perfect and completely happy, there was nothing it needed. Yet out of its goodness it chose to create and all it willed came into being. . . . One after another the Spirit made the light, the stars, the sky, and the Earth with its plants and animals. Last of all, the Spirit made Humans.*

To this point, the story reads much like the biblical story from Genesis. It is the Judaeo-Christian version of the universal creation myth found in most of the world's major religions. Then, Mario shifts gears just slightly and begins to introduce the notion of the physical and scientific laws by which the Universe is governed.

> *Can we imagine animals and plants and rocks obeying the Great Spirit? The animals do not understand when we talk to them, so could they be obedient? Or the winds and the sea and the mountains? You can shout and scream and wave your arms at them, but they cannot hear you for they are not even alive and they certainly won't obey you.*
>
> *Yes, that is how it seems to us. But, as you shall see, everything that exists, whether it has life or not, in all that it does and by the very fact of being there actually obeys the will of the Great Spirit.*
>
> *The Spirit's creatures do not know that they are obeying. Those that are inanimate just go on existing, those that have life move and go on living. Yet every time a cool wind brushes your cheek, its voice, if we could hear it, is saying, "Great Spirit, I obey."*

Mario goes on to talk about every creature on Earth obeying—obeying the laws of physics and chemistry established by the Creator. This is the basic mythological/scientific principle on which the whole rest of the story is founded: everything on Earth, in fact everything in the Universe, obeys the laws of nature.

So far, the story has been told only in words, offered to the children with great solemnity. Now, as Mario turns to the very origins of the Universe itself and the story of the Big Bang, the story is dramatized by actions and experiments which accompany the words. Materials for these demonstrations are often covered with black cloth to increase the sense of mystery and wonder, and they are slowly unveiled and shown to the children as the story progresses.

> *At first, there was chaos, and darkness was on the face of the deep. The Great Spirit said: "Let there be light." (a single candle is lit in the darkened room) . . . There appeared something like a vast fiery cloud which included all the stars that are in the sky: the whole Universe was in that cloud and among the tiniest of stars was our own world. But there were not stars then; as yet there was nothing except light and heat. . . . As this cloud of light and heat moved through the empty space, little drops fell from it, as when you swing some water out of a glass: some of it holds together and the rest breaks up in little drops. The countless hosts of stars are like those little drops.*

Thus, he ushers in the Big Bang with the image of droplets of water spreading throughout space. He talks about the vast distances of space and the concept of light years. He compares the number of stars to grains of sand that would cover England to a depth of 200 meters. To put *us* in perspective, he continues:

> *One of these stars, one of the grains of sand among those thousands of billions of grains of sand, is our Sun, and one millionth part of this grain is our Earth. An invisible speck of nothingness.*

Here is shown the first of a series of charts developed by Mario, this one depicting the Sun, with a tiny speck off to the side to represent the Earth. Then he returns to the theme of obedience to the laws of the Universe.

> *Every scrap of the Universe, every speck which we might think too tiny to matter, was given a set of rules to follow. To the little particles which are like smoke . . . the Spirit said: as you become cold you shall come closer and become smaller. . . . The particles assumed different states which are called the solid, the liquid, and the gaseous state.*

As Mario continues the discussion of these various states of matter, the text is accompanied by a series of demonstrations or experiments to illustrate what is being said — a tray of three beakers containing ice, water, and air; a jar full of ball bearings to show how the molecules move around each other; a Bunsen burner to turn the solids of ice, crayon, and solder to liquid and then to gas, and to demonstrate the different rates at which these changes occur in different substances.

A teacher presents an experiment on density and gravity during the telling of the Creation Story to a group of students.

The laws are still expressed in mythological terms as "obedience to the Great Spirit's will," but the demonstrations have moved into the realm of science. The text and the charts and the experiments continue until the conclusion:

> *Rocks, water, air: solids, liquids, gases. Today, as it was yesterday and millions of years ago, the Great Spirit's laws are obeyed in the self-same way . . . the Earth and all the elements and compounds it is made of, as they fulfill their task, whisper with one voice: "Great Spirit, Thy will be done: we obey."*

This dramatic, yet simple story of the creation is the impressionistic lesson which lays the foundation for a whole series of experiments and activities through which the children can explore the world of science. This is the pattern of the Montessori elementary curriculum — story, then study.

For some, the biblical overtones of Mario Montessori's story of the "God Who Has No Hands" can serve to allay fears that we are somehow doing away with divine creation by talking about the Big Bang and the evolution of the cosmos. All but the most literal interpretations of the biblical accounts allow for a scientific view of creation that is in harmony with the religious viewpoint.[57] Certainly, Teilhard de Chardin—dedicated paleontologist and faithful Jesuit priest—saw no contradiction between evolution and the biblical creation accounts.

For others, the references to God and biblical overtones pose a stumbling block for classroom use in a secular society which values the separation of church and state as an inviolable principle. Some Montessori educators have adapted the idea of Mario Montessori's story of creation and written their own versions which eliminate references to God while still preserving the drama of the story. That can range from a simple substitution of "Great Spirit" for God, as we have done in this book, to a completely new story which eliminates all references to a divine power.

There are other versions of the story available to the Montessori teacher. One of the best for use in the classroom is that of Jennifer Morgan called *Born With a Bang: The Universe Tells our Cosmic Story.* This beautifully illustrated book is the first of a trilogy matching three Great Lessons of Montessori— the Story of Creation, the Story of Life, and the Story of Humans.

The book is wonderfully resourced and faithful to modern science, telling of the details about the emergence of the first particles after the Big Bang, the first atoms, the formation of stars, galaxies, supernovas, the solar system, and our Earth. What makes all this science accessible to children is the way Morgan gives the information in the context of a story involving the Universe telling the child of how it dreamed, changed, and evolved to make the child possible—the ultimate story behind where we come from as humans.

In the back of the book there are notes on the scientific concepts contained in the story, a timeline, a glossary, and a list of resources, all useful tools for the Montessori teacher.

Another great resource designed for giving young children access to the stories of the Universe, life, and humans is a trilogy of rhyming comic books by a talented young artist-illustrator named James Lu Dunbar. With a passion

---

57 See the postscript at the end of Chapter 2 for a fuller discussion of this controversy.

for science and an eye for making science fun, Dunbar has produced three books in the "Universe Verse" series—*Bang!*, *It's Alive!*, and *Great Apes!* (he finished the last one in 2013). He is using Kickstarter to fund a goal of making PDF coloring-book style versions of the series available for free download (enter James Lu Dunbar in Google for more information about him and his series).

Swimme and Berry, in *The Universe Story*, have written a nine-page prologue[58] that beautifully summarizes and dramatizes the entire cosmogenesis, the birth and evolutionary unfolding of the Universe itself. It begins 15 billion years ago when the Universe "flared forth," continues through the formation of the galaxies, and the creative explosions of the supernovas. The authors give mythical names to the life forms that eventually emerged on the planet Earth, beginning with Aries, the first living cell; Vikengla, the first eukaryote; and Argos, the first multicellular animal. Human history is placed in the context of this evolutionary story, from the first hominids and toolmakers, through the Neolithic villages, and into the urban centers of the Great Civilizations.

Their version of the Creation Story covers the entire Montessori cultural curriculum and is an ideal resource for combining modern discoveries in space with conventional Cosmic Education. To use it in the classroom, the Montessori teacher must rephrase it from the essentially adult language of the original into words that can be understood by six-year-olds. Furthermore, it may be necessary to personalize the characters of the story with humanlike features to make it into a "story" format suitable for this young audience. Finally, there is a need for more than words—something along the lines of the experiments from the traditional Montessori presentation—to illustrate the words and dramatize the story.

Any creation story used in the classroom should have the accuracy of modern science, the mythic and poetic appeal of the ancient creation stories of the Native Americans,[59] and the opportunity for opening connections to the studies embodied in the rest of the Montessori curriculum. Whether the

---

58 Swimme and Berry, *The Universe Story*, p. 7–15.

59 There are many collections of creation stories or origin tales available to the teacher. Among them are David Leeming's *A Dictionary of Creation Myths*; Virginia Hamilton's *In The Beginning: Creation Stories from Around the World*; Michael Caduto and Joseph Bruchac's *Keepers of Life, Keepers of the Earth*, and *Keepers of the Animals*; Richard Erdoes and Alfonso Ortiz's *American Indian Myths and Legends*; and C.J. Taylor's *How We Saw the World* and *Bones in a Basket*.

original Mario Montessori story or a different version is used, the important point is to preserve the element of story. It is the story that provides the impression, creates the overview to serve as context for understanding, and sets the hook that lures the child into the studies that follow.[60]

The story of the birth of the Universe is the chapter in the complete narrative that has undergone the greatest elaboration in the past half century, and it is important for Montessori teachers to be aware of some of the story elements available to them. The understanding of the Big Bang has been expanded greatly by such scientific instruments as the Hubble Telescope and the Large Hadron Collider, the largest and most complex piece of scientific equipment in the world, on the border of France and Switzerland.

These have helped scientists take pictures far back in time—to the 300,000-year-old infancy of the Universe—and to recreate conditions in the early Universe to detect the emergence of the first sub-atomic particles of matter. These and other advances in the fields of astronomy and cosmology have fleshed out the details of how the Big Bang unfolded in time, and the conclusions of those findings are summarized in the following story:

> *As we move back in time from the first atoms to just after the Big Bang, we move through four eras in order.*
>
> - *The Quark Era, named for elementary particles of matter.*
> - *The Hadron Era, named for heavy composite particles of protons and neutrons.*
> - *The Lepton Era, named for lightweight particles, including electrons.*
> - *The Radiation Era, named for the photons/light energy that dominated before the formation of the first atoms.*
>
> *Because changes at the sub-atomic level occur at dazzling speed, what happens in micro-seconds is equivalent to geological periods in Earth time.*
>
> *The Quark Era, which began just picoseconds (trillionths of a second) after the Big Bang, is dominated by elementary particles formed in the*

---

[60] We discovered several books that tell the story of the Big Bang in illustrations and simple text designed for the youngest readers. Three of the best for classroom use are Lidia Bailey's *The Big Bang: The Creation of the Universe*, Toronto: Annick Press Ltd., 1982, which is suitable for lower elementary children; Heather Cooper and Nigel Henbest's *Big Bang: The Story of the Universe*, New York: Dorling Kindersley, 1997, most suitable for upper elementary students; Jennifer Morgan's *Born With a Bang: The Universe Tells Our Cosmic Story*, Nevada City, CA: Dawn Publications, 2002.

transformation of pure energy into matter, according to Albert Einstein's famous equation E = mc². Those elementary particles were unable to bind together because of temperatures in the newborn Universe of trillions of degrees.

By the Hadron Era, when the Universe was just microseconds old, temperatures had cooled enough to allow quarks to bind together in triplets to form protons and neutrons, the building blocks of atomic matter. Unfortunately for the new Universe, for every proton that was formed, there was an anti-proton, wiping out the new matter—almost. For every billion anti-protons, there were one billion and one protons, leading to the survival of enough protons to build the whole Universe we observe today.

Because there were so many more lightweight particles, like electrons, than heavy particles like protons and neutrons, the next era—lasting for the first ten seconds of the Universe—is called the Lepton Era. Once again, there were anti-electrons to cancel out the electrons—except for that one-in-a-billion difference.

Finally came the Radiation Era, which lasted 300,000 years. Photons, or packages of light energy formed in the war of protons and anti-protons, dominated the Universe. But this light could not escape—and be seen billions of years later on our planet—until the first true atoms were formed by the pairing of proton and electron in the hydrogen atom. At that point, the fog cleared and photons could travel in straight lines.

That event created the Cosmic Microwave Background (CMB) and offered the first picture available to us of the still relatively infant Universe—just 300,000 years out of 13.7 billion—and Penzias and Wilson won the Nobel Prize for snapping the baby's picture in the 1960s.

When this story is told to elementary-aged children, it is less important that they understand the scientific intricacies of the account than that they are left with a sense of wonder and awe at what Swimme and Berry call the marvelous "primordial flaring forth" of the Universe in the Big Bang.

That emotion is enhanced by the knowledge scientists have calculated that those tiny particles of matter would have spread out into nothingness, never moving slow enough to clump together to form stars, planets, and galaxies, if the Big Bang had been just a trillionth of a percent faster; and it would have collapsed in on itself and returned to the original point of unity if it had been just that fraction slower and less powerful.[61]

The awe and wonder generated by the scientific story of "creation" is no less powerful than readers experience from the account of Genesis. And, for believers, it only makes the act of divine creation that much more amazing and awe-inspiring.

Experiments and the Study of Science

Once students have heard the story that introduces the origin and qualities of the Universe, they are poised to pursue a series of experiments developed by Mario Montessori to illustrate and explore the Creation Story in more detail. At this point, good Montessori teachers refrain from the temptation of doing everything for the children; instead, they allow the children to experience the excitement of exploration. While traditional education leads us to think of teachers as the dispensers of all information, Montessori education tells us that we are only guides to the students' own learning process.

The experiments that follow the Creation Story are designed to elaborate on the laws of physics and chemistry which govern the whole Universe. They are carefully planned to be simple and understandable with a minimum of adult intervention. The adult sets up the materials for the experiments and composes the command cards that guide the students and, in some cases, the teacher also provides a brief demonstration of how to use the materials. The children are monitored to make sure they are using the materials safely. For the most part, however, the command cards and materials themselves provide the children with all they need for their study of some very important and fundamental scientific principles.

As the students perform these experiments, either individually or in small groups, they discover the principles underlying them and learn the vocabulary scientists have developed to explain these phenomena. For example, a

---

61 Swimme and Berry, *The Universe Story*, p. 18.

command card directing the students to separate iron filings from sand with a magnet demonstrates the concept of *mixtures*; sand and water shaken in a test tube teaches them about *suspensions*; and sugar stirred into a beaker of water shows them what happens when a mixture becomes a *solution.* If it looks like science, that's because it is. Through their own experience and a few simple scientific experiments, the children can learn in a very sensorial, hands-on way the distinction between mixture, suspension, and solution. From there, they can go on to explore *saturation* and *supersaturation*, producing some *crystals* in the process.

Other experiments, all designed to be performed by the students themselves, focus on the three states of matter—*solid, liquid,* and *gas.* A pitcher with holes in it, for example, sprays water and demonstrates the way a liquid presses downwards and sideways to fill any shape available to it. A little perfume in a cup allows the children to experience the presence of gases with their sense of smell. A steel rod, a rubber eraser, and a lump of plasticene demonstrate different types of solids and the scientific concepts behind them—*rigid, elastic,* and *plastic.* The law of gravity is demonstrated through such simple experiments as mixing oil, water, and molasses in a test tube and allowing them to separate into layers by their various densities.

These are examples of some of the science experiments done in the Montessori curriculum by lower elementary children. You may recognize them as similar to science experiments in traditional schools. What makes them different is the context in which they are performed and understood. They are not merely demonstrations of isolated principles of science. They are the study of parts of a story—the Story of the Universe. They are an exploration of the laws of the cosmos within the unifying parameters of the Creation Story.

For students developmentally ready for the "story of the birth of atoms" outlined above—either lower or upper elementary students—the study that follows the story offers many options for research and elaboration. What are some added details they could learn about each of the four eras (quark, hadron, lepton, and radiation)?

What part of the current Universe is made up of atomic matter? (Answer, only 4%, with the rest composed of Dark Matter and Dark Energy, concepts far beyond the understanding of the average elementary student—to say nothing of most of their teachers!) While the scientific understanding of such amazing facts is not the goal for elementary students, these kinds of scientific findings can produce the awe and wonder that we spoke about earlier.

When did the first stars form? How do galaxies come into being, and what shapes do they take? How did hydrogen atoms turn into helium and the rest of the elements of the periodic table? What is stellar nucleosynthesis?

STELLAR NUCLEOSYNTHESIS

Learning in Montessori is not linear but cyclical, with concepts revisited in a spiral fashion as children advance in age. For the nine- to twelve-year-old children in our upper elementary programs, the Story of the Universe can be retold within the context of stellar nucleosynthesis—the formation of complex elements by the fusion of atomic nuclei within the energy-rich environment of a star. This is simply a more sophisticated version of the Creation Story. Just as the Creation Story introduces the six- to nine-year-old child to the laws that govern the Universe, an account of star birth and death in stellar nucleosynthesis gives the older children a context in which to understand the evolutionary unfolding of the entire Universe. Here is an example of some of the language that can be used in telling this story:

> *After the initial explosion of the Big Bang some 15 billion years ago, colliding particles formed atoms of hydrogen, the first building blocks of matter as we know it. Clouds of this primitive gas filled the whole Universe, and variations in the density of the cloud allowed matter to clump into galactic clouds and eventually to form clusters of stars within those galaxies. Each star's birth and continued existence was made possible by a balance between the force of gravity drawing in all the neighboring particles of matter and nuclear explosions within the star pushing outward. The interior of each star is like a nuclear furnace in which primitive hydrogen atoms, with a single proton in each nucleus, are eventually fused*

into atoms of a new element called helium, with two protons (and two neutrons) in each nucleus—a process which releases energy equivalent to countless nuclear bombs. This is the beginning of stellar nucleosynthesis, or the ability of stars to fuse or force together the nuclei of simple atoms into new, more complicated elements.

In ordinary stars, like our own Sun, the forces of gravity and the fusion of nuclear material eventually produce elements as heavy as carbon, with six protons in each nucleus. However, such stars never get hot enough to burn the carbon, and they eventually die out and evolve into what astronomers call "white dwarfs," or tiny stars which have been packed so densely that a single spoonful of matter from such a star would weigh thousands of pounds.

In more massive stars, there is enough fuel to keep the nuclear furnace going through the production of even heavier elements such as oxygen, all the way up to iron, an extremely stable element with 26 protons. As gravity continues to draw new matter into the center of such a giant star, the pent-up energy eventually reaches a point where it explodes in a massive outburst called a supernova, generating temperatures ranging up to trillions of degrees, producing all of the heavier elements in the periodic table and spewing the products of this fusion process out into the surrounding space to form asteroids, planets, and eventually, through an evolutionary process of billions of years, life and humans.

The fascinating tale of the birth and death of stars provides the impressionistic overview that will lead to studies of physics, chemistry, and eventually, biology. This will bring the students beyond the level of learning they reached in lower elementary.

Introducing the children to stellar nucleosynthesis provides the foundation for a truly cosmic understanding of how the atoms that form the stuff of the Universe, the elementary particles that make up everything from the giant stars to the tiniest microorganism of our living planet, come from the initial, creative process of the Big Bang and its aftermath. The Story of the Earth, the Story of Life, the Story of Humans, all had their beginnings in that process. The atoms which make up the bodies of each one of us and everything around us had their beginnings billions of years ago in the explosive creation of stars. Evolution did not begin with the first life on planet Earth — the story stretches billions of years back into the past, to the moment the stars first began to form in the sky. Truly, we are made of star dust.

The account can be accompanied by a dramatization of the macrocosmic forces that created the microscopic world of atoms, with the gigantic furnaces of the stars creating the new elements of the periodic table. The children can be enlisted to act out the parts of this cosmic play, representing the forces at work within the stars with a swirling movement that forms an ever tighter circle. Or, the lesson can be presented by the Montessori teacher strictly as a gift to the children — what Maria Montessori called a first-period lesson.

It is an impressionistic presentation designed to excite the imagination and interest of the students for further exploration of the principles of the modern sciences. Swimme and Berry tell the details of this story in scientific detail, but with the poetry of mystics, in the first three chapters of *The Universe Story*.[62] They explain how the initial flaring-forth created a Universe of particles that collided and bombarded each other into nothingness in a frenzied rush. Finally, some of these particles were able to escape destruction long enough to form a lasting attraction that held together the first atoms of hydrogen, setting the stage for the ensuing story of stellar nucleosynthesis. Such a story can be used to expand the children's understanding of the laws of the Universe beyond gravity to the other three forces — electromagnetism, the weak nuclear interaction, and the strong nuclear interaction. Without attempting to reach the level of understanding of a college physics major, the students can be given an initial glimpse into the Universe on the microscopic level as well as the macroscopic level. Now, they can proceed beyond story into study, with a new context for understanding.

The study of simple machines like levers or pulleys within the discipline of physics can now be understood as one instance of the law of gravity. If students are presented an impressionistic lesson about stellar nucleosynthesis, they can be led to make the mental connection that these machines respond to the same law that led to the formation of the stars and the galaxies in the boiling cosmos, moments after the original explosion of matter some

---

62 Swimme and Berry, *The Universe Story*, p. 17–61.

15 billion years ago. How different to understand simple machines in this context than in isolation from the rest of the Universe.

The study of chemistry takes on a whole new attraction and meaning in this context, becoming in effect something we can call evolutionary chemistry. The periodic table is not just a collection of letters to connect with names of elements and scientific facts like atomic weight and periodic sequences. The elements of the periodic table are the products of star births and deaths. They are our connection to the Universe; they are a major part of the bigger story.

When we enter the realm of biology and the study of the evolution of life from the simple prokaryotes, those organisms without a defined nucleus, to the complexity of our own human species, we are not studying a phenomenon that began just a few billion years ago, within the lifetime of our planet. These organisms were made possible and began 15 billion years ago with Creation, the Big Bang, or whatever we choose to call the starting point.

Some Montessori teachers might feel inadequate to the challenge of explaining the birth and death of stars to their students. Astrophysics may not have been one of the subjects they studied in college. But there is no need to feel inadequate or to settle for less than the big story. There is a wonderful collection of resources, both for teachers and students, which can be obtained through the Astronomical Society of the Pacific, an organization founded in 1889 to increase understanding and appreciation of astronomy.[63] Among the books and videos offered by this group and elsewhere, there are several which treat the subject in ways that the average layman can understand with a little work.[64]

When students are initiated into the context of the Universe before they study such traditional subjects as physics, chemistry, and biology, they can then see these studies as vital parts of the overall story of the cosmos. This is Cosmic Education.

---

63 This organization puts out a catalog of sources including books, CD-ROMs, videos, posters, and other materials, with indications of appropriate grade levels. They can be contacted through their website at www.astrosociety.org or by calling 1-800-335-2624.

64 In addition to *The Universe Story,* there is Carl Sagan's 13-part television documentary produced for the Public Broadcasting System or his book entitled *Cosmos* (New York: Random House 1980). There is *Stephen Hawking's Universe: The Cosmos Explained* by David Filkin (New York: Basic Books 1997), based on the BBC/WNET television series. In a simpler style, there are helpful chapters in a book we have already referred to earlier—Sagan's and Ann Druyan's *Shadows of Forgotten Ancestors.*

The Timeline of the Universe

What clock do we use to measure the time of this story? Our earthly periods of years and centuries are not adequate in this context. We have to create a timeline with a scale of billions of years.

In our human-centered way of thinking, we also measure the Universe in "light years," or the distance light travels during one of our Earth years. This is primarily a measurement of immense distances, 5.9 trillion miles for each light year, allowing us to mentally touch the farthest reaches of the Universe. However, it is also an expression of time. When we view a spot in the Universe a light year away from us, we are actually "seeing" one year into the past. We see that spot as it was a year ago, not as it is now. It simply took that long for the visual sensation of that reality to reach us at the speed of light. With the power of our modern telescopes to see galaxies billions of light years away, we not only look outward to the edges of the Universe, but we see backward into the entire history of that Universe by looking directly at what was happening very close to its beginning.

Our clock for this level of history studies is measured by the evolving ages of an expanding Universe and the life cycle of the stars. We can measure this in billions of years or in more complicated concepts like that of light years. Our minds stumble over the time/distance relationships involved here, but our personal history must be seen against the backdrop of the stars to be properly understood.

Although Maria and Mario Montessori did not pass down timelines for this part of the story to be used in the classroom, Montessori teachers can develop their own timelines with the children in their classes. Timelines, or linear representations of the passage of time and changing events, are a fixture in every Montessori classroom. But they don't have to come ready-made off the shelf. Why not work with the students in our classes to make one for this part of the story as well, one that is measured in billions of years and whose last third can be "stretched out" later to show the life of the Earth? The timeline in the back of *The Universe Story*, or any similar source, can be used as a guideline.

Conclusion

We have attempted to explain in this chapter how Cosmic Education is carried out in Montessori classrooms with the part of the curriculum dealing with the Creation Story/stellar nucleosynthesis and the resulting studies of physics, chemistry, and biology. The study is done within the context of the story. It is only against the backdrop of the Universe itself that these studies can be properly understood.

This is what Maria Montessori believed about Cosmic Education. This is the vision that guides us in our education of the children in our care. When we teach physics, we do so against the backdrop of the laws which govern the stars themselves; when we teach chemistry, we explain the origin of the elements in the giant, explosive processes of stellar nucleosynthesis; when we teach geology, we situate that study in the context of the formation of the pieces of the Universe itself; when we study biology, we show its start in the powerful energy displayed in the birth of the stars and our sun; when we study anthropology and history, we see the human species as a product of the evolutionary process that began billions of years ago with the Big Bang itself.

Cosmic Education puts everything in its place within the whole, the cosmos. It gives meaning to everything, including our own lives as humans. As Montessori educators, we teach spirituality without teaching religion, bringing children into touch with the ineffable principles or "Spirit" which make the Universe a unified whole.[65] We introduce young children to the most sophisticated philosophical concepts ever conceived by the human mind, encouraging them to pursue the truly big questions in life. We tap into the mystical experience of being a part of the cosmos and help our students realize that they are truly children of the Universe.

---

65 Spirituality, for people of faith, consists of a belief in a divine being as the foundation of all existence. A more humanistic definition of spirituality recognizes the pervasive influence of energy forces which elude full human explanation. A Montessori teacher does not need to ascribe to or be a proponent for either viewpoint over the other. However, as Aline D. Wolf argued in her book *Nurturing the Spirit*, an authentic Montessori education implies some form of spirituality.

The Story of the Universe

The Story of the Stars and the Solar System

Physics & Chemistry
Metaphysics & Astronomy

Chapter 5

The Story of the Solar System

THE NEXT SEGMENT OF the Montessori curriculum, the second circle inward, is completely contained in that of the Universe, and it focuses on the closer reality of the formation of the galaxies, the stars, and our solar system within that Universe. This constitutes a new chapter in the Epic of Evolution. This part of the story reviews some of the same ground as the previous Story of the Universe, but it centers on the particular star which is our Sun and the formation of the planets in the solar system.

In Montessori classes, teachers do not usually tell this story as one separate from the Creation Story. There is a great leap in time and context between the Story of the Universe and the Story of Life, the first two Great Lessons of the classic Montessori canon. Some upper elementary classrooms fill in part of the narrative with the introduction of stellar nucleosynthesis, as described in the previous chapter. However, there is no great lesson, no major area of the Montessori curriculum for younger elementary children devoted exclusively to the portion of the story dealing with our solar system, except the studies on Sun and Earth. Those are studies rather than story; the story is essentially missing unless the teacher fills in the blanks.

Furthermore, these younger children need a little more background on the stars to understand the formation of our star, the Sun, and the rest of the solar system. The relationship between the Sun and the Earth is certainly critical for an understanding of our planet and the eventual development of life. To know "who we are," we must study this critical and vital relationship. However, children need to know what came before our Sun and planets. If they spend some time studying the formation of the galaxies, the life cycles of the stars, and their contribution to the evolutionary story, they will have a fuller answer to the question "Where do I come from?" Our Sun did not just appear in the sky from the first moment after the Big Bang. It is a descendant of 10 billion years of creativity. And we humans do not have just a metaphorical link with the stars; we are descendants of the life cycle of the stars in a real, physical sense.

The story on which this study is based is already embedded by implication in the Creation Story, and Montessori teachers can refer back to this original story to lay the foundation for the study of Sun and Earth. Or, if they want to do something more specific than the Creation Story, they can adapt an already existing story like the one in Jennifer Morgan's *Born with a Bang* or the prologue of Swimme and Berry's *The Universe Story* to build an impressionistic lesson. Or they can do some research, use a bit of creativity, and compose a new story to introduce the study of Sun and Earth.

Teachers should not be afraid to develop their own "great lessons" to complement the Montessori repertoire of stories. In our own time, we have the advantage of decades of actual space exploration and astronomical studies that Montessori did not experience. That perspective can be used for the benefit of our children, to let them experience their identity as children of the Universe in ways even Montessori could not have known. The following is our version of a possible story for younger elementary children, based on the current understanding of science. It can be changed to meet the situation of a particular teacher or class of children, and dramatizations of the main points will enhance its effectiveness.

The Story of the Stars and our Sun

Fifteen billion years ago, before the Big Bang—in fact, before there was such a thing as time—there were no stars in the sky, no light in the Universe, no Universe at all. In this time before time, there was nothing we could have seen with our eyes or heard with our ears or smelled with our noses. Of course, we weren't there at all 15 billion years ago. The Earth had not yet formed. In fact, there were no planets, no stars, no asteroids, no space. There was just . . . nothing.

This part of the story could be told in a darkened classroom, with the children asked to be as quiet as possible with their eyes closed to eliminate other sensations.

Out of this nothingness, in a mysterious way that we humans cannot understand, the whole Universe suddenly burst into existence in what we have named the Big Bang. The Big Bang was probably not an explosion like a gigantic bomb, with noise and fire and light; rather, it was an outburst of pure energy into space that only gradually changed into matter. Somehow, all the sextillion particles in the existing Universe were set in motion by that explosion of energy, crashing into each other in a great rush to move out into a "space" they could call their own.

As we learned in the Creation Story, many of these particles were so attracted to each other by the force of gravity that they joined together. In fact, if they had been moving just a little bit faster, they would eventually have moved out of reach of each other and never come together to form the stars or the planets. Or, if they had been moving just a little bit slower, the pull of gravity would have sucked them up like a giant vacuum cleaner and pulled all the particles back into a space without space—back into nothingness. As it was, they were moving at just the right speed to eventually settle down and gather together into colonies of matter, great swirling clouds of particles.

To dramatize this portion of the story, arrange the children in a line, joined by their fingers to each other. As a first demonstration, move the line faster and faster around the room so that the children on the end inevitably lose their grip and break off from the chain. Next, slow down the front of the line so those in the back collide and bunch together with those in the front. Finally, show the perfect equilibrium by having the children move in a slow spiral.

> *This all happened in the blink of an eye, a split second after the Big Bang. Within a matter of minutes, the first permanent gatherings of particles began to form into hydrogen and helium, the first real elements in the Universe, the building blocks of everything that was to come after them. These building blocks were so small that they would have only been able to be seen with a microscope if we had been there. Yet, from these tiny collections of particles, over billions of years, giant galaxies with billions of enormous stars were born.*

This would be a good place to show a photo of a galaxy. NASA is a wonderful resource for actual pictures of things we formerly represented with drawings. Just go to their website[66] for a wealth of information and visual materials. Teachers can either download the pictures, purchase full poster size pictures, or show the pictures through a computer projector if the school has the required technology. Also, to continue the active involvement of the students in the dramatization, students can hold signs identifying them as protons, neutrons, and electrons and then join hands in the proper proportions to symbolize hydrogen and helium.

> *As these giant gatherings of hydrogen and helium began to collapse inward, they formed stars, which were like immense furnaces of nuclear power. As these furnaces burned hotter and brighter, the stars ran the risk of collapsing into nothingness again. To survive, some of them combined particles of hydrogen and helium into new substances like carbon and other more solid elements. Some of these stars just didn't have enough energy to survive and they died anyway, collapsing into the cinder of a black hole that no longer burned with the brilliance of a star. This collapse, however, also produced something new, something we call a supernova, an explosion of elementary particles out into space. Carbon, oxygen, nitrogen, and dozens of other elements spewed out in all directions, eventually joining other particles to create new stars and planets.*

66 www.NASA.gov

Another opportunity exists here for a dramatic photo of a supernova explosion from NASA or some other source. There are wonderful books on astronomy loaded with actual photos taken with modern telescopes that can provide these illustrations. Also, to continue the dramatization, the children can hoist their signs and join hands to form new combinations to represent carbon and other elements.

> *This cycle of star birth and creative death went on for billions of years. Finally, about five billion years ago, there was a supernova explosion in the Orion arm of the Milky Way Galaxy. That supernova produced the matter for a new star, our Sun, one of the estimated 400 billion stars in the Milky Way. Our Sun is an impressive sight—a seething hot ball of burning gas, thousands of degrees at the surface area we call the photosphere and millions of degrees in the gas cloud surrounding the surface we call the chromosphere. The Sun is so hot that it spews out vast streams of particles in what is called a solar wind. Yet, there's nothing special about our Sun compared to the billions of other stars, aside from the fact that it is close enough for us to see as more than a dot in the sky and it is the energy source for life on our home planet.*

Now is a good time to study this part of the sky in an astronomical chart featuring Orion and then to show the children a NASA photo of the Sun's explosive surface.

> *Around this special star we call our Sun, other particles of matter swirled together into all the planets of our solar system, some of them rocky balls of metal and minerals, and others dense clouds of poisonous gases. These balls of rock and gas circle the Sun in a sort of cosmic dance, turning on their own axes and twirling in elliptical patterns around the dance master, the Sun. Mercury, the innermost planet, made of rock, is only 35 million miles away from the Sun and makes a complete circle around the dance master in just a few Earth months. The most distant planet, Neptune, is composed mostly of gas and is some 2.8 billion miles from the Sun; it takes about 165 Earth years to complete its elliptical orbit. In between are the rocky planets of Earth, Venus, and Mars, and the gigantic gas balls of Jupiter, Saturn, and Uranus. These planets of*

gas are so huge that they have attracted dozens of moons or satellite balls of matter, some of them bigger than our own Moon.

At this point, show the children a diagram of the planets, in relative size and with names, so they can distinguish the rocky planets from the gaseous ones. Individual planets can be shown from NASA pictures as well, replacing drawings with actual photos. Or, to keep the active dramatization going, distribute new signs among the students to represent the planets in their relative sizes. Explain to the children that the size of the Sun (one million times bigger than the Earth) cannot be portrayed in accurate proportion to the planets because it would be too big to fit in the classroom, the all purpose room, or even the playground. Line up the children carrying the signs in the order described above and have them encircle the sign that represents the Sun.

One of the rocky planets—the third one out from the Sun—is our own planet Earth. It is almost 8,000 miles in diameter, making it the largest of the rocky planets, and it follows an elliptical path around the Sun at a distance of some 93 million miles.

Now show a NASA photo of planet Earth taken from the moon. What an awesome sight to see our own planet from the perspective of space! With an actual photograph, we can see the thin blue layer of atmosphere and variegated surface we call the Biosphere.

In each of our Earth days, our planet makes a pirouette around its own axis. And in each of our Earth years, it completes one journey around the Sun, causing seasons to change as the Sun's rays are affected by the tilt of the Earth in relation to the Sun.

This is the time to show the children some of the traditional Sun and Earth demonstrations, in brief fashion the way the experiments were introduced in the Creation Story. A globe and a bare light in a darkened room are all that is needed, with the globe turning on its own axis, to show how the Earth faces toward the Sun and away from it to produce day and night. The same materials can be used to show how the Earth moves around the Sun in the course of a year, with the tilt of the planet producing the seasons. Here, use the Montessori charts to illustrate these points for the children.

In addition to creating night and day and the seasons of the year, these movements of our planet on its own axis and around the Sun cause different parts of our planet to have different climates. The poles, those parts which are furthest away from the direct rays of the Sun, remain cold and frozen throughout the whole year, while the belt we call the equator around the middle of the Earth sizzles with heat. This divides our planet into different zones we call torrid, temperate, and frigid.

Here, the children can be shown other charts of the Montessori Sun and Earth curriculum.

This is the story of how our Earth was born, of how the evolving Universe made it possible for our planet to form some five billion years ago. This is the start of a new chapter in Universe history that eventually led to the emergence of life and our own species upon the planet. It was only because of those billions of years of star life and death that the fragile conditions for life were created on this speck of rock we call home. We are children of the Universe.

Such a story, or one like it, can be used to introduce the usual Montessori studies on Sun and Earth and provide the material for a new timeline as well. If it can be made dramatic and impressionistic by the classroom teacher, it will be an attractive hook to lure the student into these studies and fill in some blanks in the telling of the story of our cosmic past.

Sun and Earth Studies

The study which follows such a story can include new, teacher-made or purchased materials on the life and death of the stars, the various types of stars or stages in their existence, and an overview of the stars we see in the sky at different times of the year. These materials, which can be obtained in educational supply stores or from science education catalogs, can be made available for the students to study on their own.

Many Montessori classrooms already include studies of the solar system and the planets. These are particularly appropriate in light of the wonderful advances in our knowledge of the planets through the American space program, the amazing photos available from NASA for our study, and the opportunity to take class field trips to space centers and museums. Furthermore, there is a noble purpose for these studies. They help us better understand and appreciate our own planet, leaving us in awe of the delicate balance of forces that makes Earth a green, living planet, while the other planets are scorched balls of lifeless rock or cold masses of swirling poisonous gas. In a word, they help us better understand who we are.

Finally, the materials familiar to all Montessori classrooms in this area are those on Sun and Earth. They appeal to the imagination of the student to master an understanding of the dance that takes place between these two celestial bodies. If presented with the right degree of scientific understanding and appreciation for the delicate fragility of the arrangement, they can produce a sense of awe within the students and another step toward understanding our origins and our place in space.

As designed in the classic Montessori curriculum, these are not self-guided studies. Rather, they are true presentations by the teacher, to be followed by activities on the part of the students. With the complexity of information contained in these studies, some guidance on the part of the teacher in the form of a transmission of information is necessary for understanding. However, if some of that information is imparted during an elaborate telling of the story, as suggested above, it should be possible to leave more of the study to the stu-

Two girls work on Sun and Earth studies, with the girl in front using a chart showing temperature zones and the one in the back a chart on the equinoxes and solstices.

dents themselves. To further guide this study, teachers can provide a set of command cards like the ones used for the science experiments following the Creation Story.

The first series of studies has to do with the movement of the Earth around the Sun. By expanding on what they already know from the Creation Story, students take a closer look at the concepts of gravity and centrifugal force, the opposing forces that bring particles together and pull them apart. They take a washer tied to a string, spin it around, and draw the string in through the center of a spool to represent the inward pull of the Sun's gravity; they spin a bucket of water around and over their heads to illustrate centrifugal force. It is the balance between these two forces that keeps the Earth in orbit around the Sun, with the inward pull of gravity counteracting the outward pull of centrifugal force just enough to keep the Earth in its place relative to the Sun.

A series of Montessori charts and demonstrations leads the student through a study of the distribution of the Sun's heat on the surface of the Earth—cold at the poles and hot near the equator; an explanation of day and night, as the Earth's face turns toward or away from the Sun; of the yearly circuit of Earth around Sun, with the shifting position of the Earth's tilt producing variations of hot and cold; and of the daily ebb and flow of heat that keeps the Earth's temperature within a range that can sustain life. If anything were slightly different, we would be either crispy critters or frozen popsicles.

Then comes another series of charts and experiments with toothpicks and plasticene, flashlights and black paper, globes and lights, map strips and tiny clocks, which lead the student to an understanding of the time zones that circle the globe (allowing them to compare the time in their hometown to the time for relatives in other parts of the world); the origin of the seasons—it's all in the tilt; what happens on the summer and winter solstices and the spring and fall equinoxes; the Tropic of Cancer and the Tropic of Capricorn; and the torrid, temperate, and frigid zones of our planet.

There's a lot of advanced science contained in the Montessori presentations and experiments on Sun and Earth, as well as the extended study of the stars and planets of the solar system. The study is designed to take another step in understanding who we are and how we got here, to complete yet another chapter of the story we tell in Cosmic Education.

Timeline

There is no separate timeline in the classic Montessori repertoire for the story of the stars and solar system, although one could easily be put together with the help of resources like *The Universe Story* or other books like it. It would involve "stretching out" the latter portion of the Universe timeline created for the previous chapter.

Yet, time is very much a part of our studies of Sun and Earth already. We use the relationship between Sun and Earth to establish the clocks by which we measure our relatively short personal, national, and world histories. We count one revolution of the Earth around the Sun, the time it takes for the four seasons to pass, as a year in our measurement of time. We count the revolutions of the Moon around the Earth, watch the Sun's reflection wax and wane on the face of the Moon, and divide our year into twelve months. We time our Earth's revolution on its own axis, facing us alternately toward the Sun and away from it, and count that a day in time.

There are presentations in the Montessori curriculum to familiarize the children with these concepts and introduce them into the way we measure and record time on our planet. The children learn about the months of the year, the days of the week, the seasons of the year, the counting of years, and calendars. These concepts are presented in a series of lessons that examine the origin of the words, explore the history of the way we count the years, and help the children master these critical pieces of information for keeping track of daily living. They are given a taste of what the very concept of "time" means, something that until then they have not consciously studied.

Rather than teach all this material as isolated pieces of information, it can all be done within the context of the story of the stars and the solar system to give it more excitement and meaning, to make it part of Cosmic Education.

Conclusion

The Sun and Earth presentations of the Montessori curriculum provide a good guide to the study of this chapter in the Epic of Evolution, the story of the stars and the solar system within the Story of the Universe. Teachers can anchor this study in the Creation Story, or they can create a new story to introduce the study as we have suggested. They can develop a timeline to illustrate this new story. Finally, they can extend the study of Sun and Earth to a study of all the planets of our solar system, perhaps providing a suitable extension for the upper elementary curriculum.

History is both time and story, and the study of science should also be rooted in story. There is room for development of story and timeline to enhance the elegance of the Sun and Earth studies already provided in the Montessori curriculum.

The Story of the Universe

The Story of the Stars and the Solar System

The Story of the Earth

Geology & Geography
Physics & Chemistry
Metaphysics & Astronomy

Chapter 6

The Story of the Earth

The third circle inward in the Epic of Evolution deals with the Story of the Earth. Our "ego-centric" way of viewing reality leads us to focus our attention on the third rock from the sun as the most important piece of the Universe to study.

Here again, there is no "great lesson," no separate story in the classic Montessori curriculum to introduce the students' study. The Creation Story provides elements that can be referred to as an introduction to these studies. Also there are passages in Maria Montessori's own words in *To Educate the Human Potential* which sing the praises of the formation of the Earth.[67]

Jennifer Morgan's trilogy offers a wonderful version of this story that begins at the end of the first book, *Born with a Bang,* and continues in the beginning of the second book, *From Lava to Life: The Universe Tells Our Earth Story.* This book too is beautifully illustrated, based on sound, up-to-date science, and told in story fashion. It is accessible to the youngest of our elementary children and stimulating as well to the oldest of our elementary students.

Or, as with the stars and solar system, teachers can be more ambitious and create their own story, a new chapter of the Universe Story, to serve as an impressionistic, introductory presentation that will capture the imagination of the children and provide them a cosmic context in which to study our

---

67   Maria Montessori, *To Educate,* Chapter 6, p. 43 ff.

planet. We suggest that students would benefit from inserting these studies into a meaningful story context, and it would allow them to pursue their study of this area more independently than commonly done in Montessori classrooms.

Creating a Story of the Earth

There are probably some geologists who wax poetic over the story of the formation of the Earth; so, there may already be a great story out there waiting to be told to the students without further elaboration. Or, the ambitious Montessori teacher with a flair for drama may create one. As we said earlier, Montessori's Great Lessons should be a model and a challenge to those who follow, not a restrictive, dogmatic recipe for all lessons. The following is just one way the story could be told:

A long, long time ago, in fact about five billion years ago, Mother Earth was just being born out of the clouds of debris and gas floating around the newborn Sun. She was born as a sphere of rock and molten metal some 8,000 miles in diameter. Like most of the collections of matter in the Universe, colossal forces of gravitation pulled together particles from a spiraling nebula into a spherical shape, while the inward compression of those elements created explosive forces which pressed outward and kept the Earth from collapsing into nothingness. The delicate balance between gravitation and explosive energy allowed Mother Earth to exist.

In the beginning, Father Fire was the unchallenged force within the newborn planet. He heated the surface of the globe to a super-hot 3,600 degrees Fahrenheit, and he caused gigantic explosions of volcanic activity that made the surface a constantly changing cauldron so hot that not even rocks could remain in a solid state and no life as we know it could exist. In addition to causing these explosions from within Mother Earth, Father Fire also sent a display of fireworks across the horizon, streaking lightning bolts that split the sky. The atmosphere was a constant display of lightning and rolling thunderstorms that shook the new planet from above.[68]

---

68 Swimme and Berry, in *The Universe Story*, refer to this phenomenon as ur-lightning, p. 85.

THE STORY OF THE EARTH   75

Artists' renditions of this stage of the planet can be found in books on geology or in poster-size format in natural history museum gift shops. Websites which provide illustrations could be projected on a screen. Finally, the model volcano that is so popular with children in the presentation of the Montessori Creation Story can be used here to illustrate the new story and make a connection with the old one.

> *For the first few hundred million years, the newborn Mother Earth was bombarded with meteors and asteroids the size of small planets, keeping her surface in constant turmoil. Finally, the collisions slowed enough to allow the planet and Father Fire to settle down. The thousands of volcanoes that kept the surface of the planet a liquid mass of molten rock began to cool enough to allow a thin crust to form on the surface, as though Mother Earth was finally able to grow a skin. This crusty skin, as thin as six miles in some places, covered a seething interior, still ruled by Father Fire. The first layer inside the crust was a 1,800-mile-thick mantle of molten rock and minerals, mostly iron and magnesium, at temperatures as high as 7,500 degrees Fahrenheit. Inside the mantle was a double core—a mixture of liquid sulfur and oxygen about 1,400 miles thick, and solid iron and nickel about 750 miles thick. Mother Earth's insides were still alive with fire and energy during the long period of Earth's history called the Archean Eon.*

This would be a good place to illustrate the parts of the Earth by cutting an onion in half, peeling the layers apart, dipping each layer in food coloring and using the sections to paint concentric circles representing the various layers of the Earth. Teachers can also show the students some of the Montessori charts from the Composition of the Earth studies to explain the layers of the Earth and lay the groundwork for their later study.

> *All this activity of Mother Earth and Father Fire produced an offspring, a shroud of gases surrounding the planet called Brother Air. Some 4 billion years ago, Brother Air, or what we call the atmosphere, was just a baby composed primarily of carbon dioxide. There were also significant quantities of hydrogen and nitrogen present, but there was no oxygen to nourish any animal life. Clouds of carbon dioxide blanketed the entire surface of Mother Earth, much like we see on the planet Venus today.*

Perhaps the students could be shown an artist's rendition of this stage of Earth next to a NASA photo of Venus for comparison. Also, there are the Montessori charts showing the layers of the atmosphere, the Earth's protective blanket.

> *After some time, Mother Earth and Father Fire belched water vapor into the atmosphere, giving birth to yet another offspring, Sister Water. In her infancy, she was nothing but a rising cloud of fog. But as she grew bigger and rose higher, she cooled in the breezes of the upper atmosphere and fell back down as torrential rains. The surface of Mother Earth was still so hot that the rains of Sister Water evaporated as soon as they hit the surface. After millions of years of this process, however, pools of water began to collect on the crusty surface, eventually forming mighty oceans that covered nearly the entire surface of the planet. It was in this soupy mixture of primitive chemicals that the first signs of life began to appear on Mother Earth.*

At this point, students could be shown a sponge globe, dripping with water. Or there may be some artist's illustrations of this stage of the planet in a geology book or on an Internet website.

> *Father Fire retreated further inside and Mother Earth's surface cooled even more. Brother Air changed from the poisonous clouds of dying volcanoes to a mixture of new and friendlier gases, while Sister Water continued to nurture the new forms of life within her oceans. Huge quantities of carbon dioxide from Brother Air were absorbed into the waters where green plants learned how to photosynthesize, capturing the energy of the Sun to make food for themselves and other living creatures. By 3.5 billion years ago, carbon dioxide had been replaced by nitrogen as the dominant gas in the atmosphere. By 1.5 billion years ago, carbon dioxide had been reduced to just a small fraction of the atmosphere, nitrogen's dominance grew, and oxygen had become a major component of Brother Air. He was now friendly for animals to breathe, and the Earth moved into the time period we call the Proterozoic Eon.*

New charts could be made to show the changes in the composition of the atmosphere. This also is an opportunity to introduce some of the charts and

THE STORY OF THE EARTH

illustrations from the Montessori studies on the Work of Water. However, these maps represent the present-day location of the continents instead of the level of continental development at this stage in the story. It would be preferable to show the Earth's surface as scientists imagine it might have been a billion years ago and emphasize the oceans as sources of new life.

> *Meanwhile, mountains formed on the crusty surface of Mother Earth. Some of them grew from volcanic flows that Father Fire built up into cone-shaped mountains. Some were pushed up from beneath the surface by rock layers pushing against other layers of rock. Some of the pushing and shoving created peaks that rose miles into the air and long chains of mountain ridges that ran for thousands of miles. For example, the towering Himalaya Mountains were formed when a section of the Earth's crust called a tectonic plate carrying present-day India collided with one carrying Eurasia. The folding and wrinkling of Mother Earth's skin as she began to show her age occurred even beneath the surface of the water, where mountain ranges cover the floor of the oceans.*

Charts in the Montessori repertoire show the types of mountain formations and hands-on materials illustrate the movement of masses of rock and fault lines. For the suboceanic mountains, topographical maps of the ocean floors can be found in most atlases which show these underwater mountain ranges.

> *Other changes were taking place in the land masses on Mother Earth. About 200 million years ago, there were no continents as we know them, just a single mass of rock geologists have named the supercontinent Pangaea, surrounded by a single ocean called Panthalassa. By about 135 million years ago, Pangaea shifted, moved and broke into two big pieces that formed Laurasia to the north (including North America, Europe, and most of Asia) and Gondwanaland in the south (including South America, Africa, India, Antarctica, and Australia). By 65 million years ago, South America had become a giant island, India drifted towards Asia, and Oceania began to break apart from Antarctica, heading toward the configuration of continents we know today. The familiar face of Mother Earth that we know took hundreds of millions of years to form.*

Illustrations of this phenomenon of continental drift are readily available in geology books or on websites on the Internet. A teacher could even use loose map pieces of the continents from Montessori materials to show how the configurations of the continents shifted during these last 200 million years.

> *The Story of the Earth is a living story. Even before life as we know it emerged, the planet Earth was alive with seething energy. Today, Earth continues to change and evolve like a living organism. Pools of molten rock break through the surface as new volcanoes and earthquakes caused by collisions of continental plates shake the ground so violently that manmade buildings tumble to the ground in pieces. Mother Earth has always been and is still "alive," moving and changing and creating herself anew each day. The four material substances—Earth, Fire, Air, Water—are still the basic source of life for all of us today.*

With the proper research of geology and other sciences and a sense of drama and creativity that can turn science into poetry, Montessori teachers can provide children with their own "great lesson" based on the life of the planet itself, adding yet another chapter in the story of Cosmic Education. Fill the story with science, tell it with poetry, and visualize it with drama so as to really "impress" the children and prepare them for study.

Studies about the Earth

Whether the Montessori teacher chooses to refer back to the Creation Story, or she creates her own imaginative story of the living planet Earth, there are study areas in the Montessori curriculum that fit into this chapter of the story. The principal ones are called Composition of the Earth, the Work of Wind, and the Work of Water. Like the Sun and Earth studies, these were usually considered to be teacher presentations followed by work on the part of the students. However, with the introduction of many of the core concepts in the course of telling the story, as above, and the creation of a new set of command cards, these can become materials for student study rather than teacher presentation.

THE STORY OF THE EARTH

The series of lessons on the Composition of the Earth begin with the "onion world" study comparing the inner and outer core, mantle, crust, and atmosphere of the Earth to the layers of the onion. Then, there are charts showing the layers and a core sample "composition strip." Other charts show an elaboration on the Earth's atmospheric blanket and its own layers. Finally, there are charts and activities to explain the formation of mountains, fault lines, and volcanoes.

In Work of Wind, there are experiments to show how air occupies space, how it rises when heated, how cool air flows in to replace the rising air, and how land both heats and cools faster than water. This leads to a series of charts illustrating the study of global wind patterns and air pressure, the effect of wind patterns on the seasons, local weather patterns, and the erosive power of winds.

It is water, however, which most attracts Maria Montessori's interest and fascination. In *To Educate the Human Potential,* Montessori talks about the work of "toiler" water, about the way it sculpts the land, the way it builds and transforms, and the way it dissolves other substances to make them more accessible and useful to living creatures.[69] It is a theme to which Montessori returns again and again in her writings, such as the chapter she dedicates to it in *From Childhood to Adolescence.*[70]

In the Montessori presentations called Work of Water, a model river trough sets the scene and shows some of the forces at work as water moves from mountain to sea.

A student lays out colored pieces of onion to represent the layers of the Earth in the Composition of the Earth study.

69 Maria Montessori, *To Educate,* p. 44–45.

70 Maria Montessori, *From Childhood,* p. 24 ff.

Maps show the location of the principal rivers of the world and the various continents, and discussions are held on the cultural significance of the rivers. Other illustrations show how rain, rivers, and oceans cause erosion that carves and molds the face of the bottles and rocks, and the massive force of glaciers. The water cycle is presented with imaginative charts on the "games of water."

For upper elementary children, extensions of these studies can be made through detailed examination of the water cycle, as well as the oxygen-carbon dioxide cycle, the nitrogen cycle, and the carbon cycle. Children can do extensive studies on weather and meteorology, ranging from setting up weather stations, to visiting TV meteorologists, to predicting the weather on their own with a few basic instruments. Detailed study of igneous, sedimentary, and metamorphic rock formations can be done, opening up the broad study area of rocks and minerals and laying the groundwork for later studies of fossils and archeology.

Once again, it is not the isolated content of these science studies that is most important for the child. Rather, the key to making these studies part of Montessori's Cosmic Education is the understanding of these fascinating phenomena within the context of the telling of the story and the realization that this is all part of the answer to the child's question of "Who am I?" "Where do I come from?" Through story and study, students learn that they are not only "children of the Universe" but, in a more specific way, they are also "children of the Earth." As the Native Americans have told us so eloquently in their culture, the Earth is truly our Mother.

Timeline

There is no timeline in the usual Montessori curriculum for this area of study, nor is one easy to construct from the presentations of Composition of the Earth, Work of Wind, and Work of Water.

However, if the Montessori teacher has been conscientious about producing timelines for the Story of the Universe and the Story of the Solar

System, another would certainly be in order for this chapter of the story. The ambition—compulsion?—that led to these earlier timelines would almost certainly have led to creation of a great story on which to build this chapter.

The material for the timeline is contained in the narrative, and teacher and children can work together on producing the timeline for the Story of the Earth. The Archean and Proterozoic Eons (sometimes called Precambrian time) together make up the first four billion years of the Earth's history. This part of the timeline should show symbolically the unfolding drama that formed the Earth as we know it today. It is only after that space of time that the eras and geological periods used on the Timeline of Life charts can be used to provide some of the terminology for the later Timeline of the Earth.

Conclusion

Whether a teacher finds satisfaction in presenting Earth studies in the context of the Creation Story, or whether story, timeline, and extensions are developed by an ambitious and creative follower of Montessori, this chapter in the story is important. It helps children to understand the sequence of events in Earth's formation, how it changed over billions of years, and how it came to provide us with the life-sustaining environment we enjoy as humans.

Another chapter has been told in the Epic of Evolution. Another step has been taken toward understanding "who we are" and discovering our cosmic task. Now, we are ready to explore the Story of Life.

The Story of the Universe

The Story of the Stars and the Solar System

The Story of the Earth

The Story of Life

Biology

Geology & Geography

Physics & Chemistry

Metaphysics & Astronomy

Chapter 7

The Story of Life

THE NEXT CIRCLE INWARD is the most fully developed in the Montessori cultural curriculum. In the Story of Life, we find another great lesson from the classic Montessori repertoire of stories. Life, that miraculous appearance of something new in the Story of the Universe, holds a fascination and attraction for children that makes it one of the primary areas of teaching in a Montessori classroom. There is a substantial body of materials to accompany the telling of the story, both from Dr. Montessori, the physician, and from her followers.

Here we come to the main chapter in the Epic of Evolution, the story of the appearance and spread of life in all its myriad forms. Here, our planet becomes home to a phenomenon not found anywhere else in the solar system and, as far as we know at present, nowhere else in the Universe. It is very unlikely that the planet Earth is the only place in the Universe where the miracle of life has emerged, but we are yet to meet any other examples of that life outside our own small speck of dust in the sky. As we look at our Earth from the perspective of outer space, it is a green planet surrounded by a life-sustaining film of blue haze—it is a miracle to behold!

In customary educational terms, the earlier chapters of the story have led to a study of astronomy (with a little metaphysics thrown in), physics and chemistry, and geology and geography. This chapter takes us into studies of history and biology.

Because of the central nature of these two subjects and the wealth of materials available in the Montessori curriculum, this chapter is different from and a bit more complicated than the ones that came before it. First, there are several versions of the story. Furthermore, the study contains elements spread throughout the curriculum, including some parts to which the children are exposed even before being told the main version of the Story of Life.

Finally, there is no set script for an original, impressionistic presentation called the Story of Life like there was for the Creation Story. Instead, Montessori teachers have several opportunities to tell the story in their own words with the Long Black Line, the Clock of Eons, and the Timeline of Life. The first belongs to the realm of pure storytelling, the second involves storytelling and timeline combined, and the third is the principal Montessori material for developing the story and studying the details. Each of these is a more detailed version of the previous one, and the final version of the story is so detailed that it cannot be told in a single lesson (although Morgan's *From Lava to Life* could be used for this purpose).

First Versions of the Story

The Long Black Line and the Clock of Eons are the first two opportunities for telling the Story of Life to the younger children in Montessori elementary. The main purpose of the Long Black Line is to impress on children the place of humans as late-comers in the tale of life, while the Clock of Eons introduces them to the divisions of Earth's history and their first timeline of life.

The Long Black Line is 30 meters of black yarn ending in a centimeter of red, wound around a spool with the red on the inside. Maria Montessori is said to have used this teaching apparatus in India to teach humility to a group of children she had observed speaking arrogantly about the age and wisdom of their culture.

The teacher, like Montessori herself, begins telling the story of our planet as she walks with the children and slowly unwinds the black yarn. She tells the children to watch the yarn carefully for a change that will indicate the appearance of human beings on the Earth. Then, depending on the preparation and storytelling ability of the teacher, the children are treated to a walk through Earth History (see the previous chapter) filled with fascinating details about the time of the volcanoes, the cooling of the planet as rains began to fall, the formation of the oceans and a crust of land, and the appearance of the first microscopic forms of life in the seas. The first part of the story uses up about half of the yarn. The teacher reminds the children to keep looking for the change of color, but there's no sign of it yet.

With the appearance of life, the storytelling shifts focus to the evolution of the first prehistoric and now extinct sea creatures, just single cells in the beginning, then ancient plants and early invertebrates, or animals without backbones.[71] There's still no sign of that special part indicating the appearance of humans. The story continues with the emergence of plants and animals onto the land, the spread of land-based amphibians, the reptiles and the reign of the dinosaurs, and finally the appearance of the first mammals. The yarn is nearly all unrolled, and the tale is almost told—but there is still no sign of humans. Finally, as the last centimeter is unrolled from the spool, the children spot the red piece indicating the appearance of humans.

What an impression! What an opportunity to present the entire story of the evolution of life on Earth and put ourselves in perspective. What a chance to move the children closer to an understanding of "who we are." Our own experience with children has been that even the youngest elementary students can appreciate this lesson, this initial telling of the Story of Life, with wonder and awe shining in their eyes.

Another opportunity to tell this chapter of the story is contained in the Clock of Eons. The same story told above with the Long Black Line can be retold as a clock is being constructed to represent the life of the Earth. An imaginary clock hand representing the passage of time from the beginning of the Earth to the present paints the hours on the clock face, starting at 12:00 and moving around the complete circle of 12 hours to the present:

- the first two hours on the clock are painted black to represent the Hadean Eon, or time that was so "hellish" with crashing asteroids and exploding volcanoes that there was no life (from 4.5 billion years ago to 3.8 billion years ago);

---

[71] Swimme and Berry tell the story of life on Earth in *The Universe Story*, Chapters 5–7, p. 81–140. A teacher could use a lot of the descriptions and information from these chapters in a classroom presentation.

- a gray section three hours long represents the Archaeon Eon, or time of "ancient life," when megamolecules formed that generated bacteria and made later life possible (from 3.8 billion to 2.5 billion years ago);
- a yellow section about five hours long represents the Proterozoic Eon, or time of "first life" as we know it, when true, eukaryotic cells were formed (from 2.5 billion years ago to 543 million years ago);
- the final two hours on the clock are called the Phanerozoic Eon, and they are further divided into subdivisions called Eras;
- a blue period 47 minutes long is called the Paleozoic Era, or time of "old life," when multicellular plants and animals evolved in the seas (from 543 million to 248 million years ago);
- a brown piece 29 minutes long represents the Mesozoic Era, or time of "middle life," when plants an the land and when amphibians and reptiles dominated the planet (from 248 million years ago to 65 million years ago);
- a green strip of just ten minutes is called the Cenozoic Era, or time of "new life," to represent the emergence of that new kind of animal called the mammal (from 65 million years ago to today);
- and finally, a thin strip of red representing a mere seventeen seconds on the clock is called the Quaternary Period or Neozoic Period, a time of "new, new life," to represent the time of humans upon the Earth (less than 2 million years).

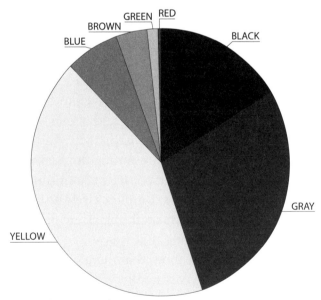

Clock of Eons - Earth Time

Another great impressionistic lesson, another opportunity for telling the Story of Life in dramatic fashion! Through these first two versions of the story, the children have become familiar with the overall story of biological evolution and learned some of the terminology they will need for the more detailed story and study they will meet in the more elaborate story connected to the Timeline of Life.

First Studies of Biology

There are numerous areas of study in biology within the Montessori curriculum directly related to the Story of Life outlined in the history presentations above. There are shelves full of materials in the typical Montessori classroom dedicated to this area, and the children's work with these materials allows them to further explore the initial telling of the story and helps prepare them for the more elaborate story in the Timeline of Life. We will describe these study areas one at a time and attempt to place them within the context of Cosmic Education.

1. External Parts of Animals and Plants

Students in a Montessori elementary classroom are introduced to the study of animals and plants as many of them are learning to read—in fact, this kind of material is a major portion of the Montessori reading program and often has been introduced to the children in the primary classes for three- to six-year-olds.

Students usually begin their studies with animals rather than plants, and with vertebrates (animals with backbones) rather than invertebrates, because these animals are more familiar to them and create a more immediate interest. However, to match the Story of Life that they may already have experienced through the Long Black Line or Clock of Eons, evolutionary sequences are followed within the study of vertebrates—fish, amphibian, reptile, bird, and mammal. Whenever possible, children study these animals initially through live examples of them in the classroom. Then they focus on their externally visible parts through a series of classified cards which include picture, label (for beginning readers), and definition (for more advanced readers). Games are made of the materials by cutting the definitions into strips to be reassembled by the students. Once the teacher has introduced the names of the external parts, most of this study is done by the students on their own, with the self-correcting feature of a control booklet (which contains all the proper information connected with the appropriate pictures).

The evolutionary sequence is also followed in a parallel study of the external parts of familiar plants—seaweed, moss, fern, conifer, and flowering plant, with the mushroom added in classrooms that have not yet converted to a five-kingdom system of classification.[72] Once again, live specimens are brought into the classroom or visited in the outdoor environment to begin the study, and classified cards are given the students to continue their studies.

2. *First Knowledge of Animals and Plants*

Next comes a series of studies called "First Knowledge" based on an initial selection of interesting animals chosen as typical examples of the classes studied under External Parts. There are pictures, labels and, in place of definition cards, mini-stories about each of the pictured plants and animals, all ending with the question: "Who am I?" Does the question sound familiar?

Then the same materials are used with a series of questions and answers to learn more about the pictured animals—In what environment or biome does the animal live? Does the animal care for its offspring? How does the animal move? How does the animal reproduce? What does the animal eat? In what climatic region does the animal live? Is the animal useful to humans? Some of the answers can be found in the "Who am I?" cards, and some must be found through research. At the end of the study, a student is able to produce a basic research report on a particular animal.

---

72   Many biologists today speak of five kingdoms for the classification of living things instead of the familiar two kingdoms of plants and animals. They separate out the Prokaryotes (sometimes called Monera and consisting mostly of Bacteria), single-celled organisms without a well-defined nucleus; Protoctista (sometimes called Protista), mostly single cells with a definite nucleus but not acting completely like either plant or animal; and Fungi (mushrooms, molds, etc.), which are unlike plants in that they don't manufacture their own food. A good source of information on this subject is Lynn Margulis's *Five Kingdoms: An Illustrated Guide to the Phyla of Life on Earth*.

There are parallel "First Knowledge" studies of a selection of plants, as well, with appropriate changes in the questions and answers.

In addition to familiarizing the children with a wealth of technical information about plants and animals that they can bring to their later studies, these exercises illustrate the similarities among all living things, a truly cosmic concept. For example, they learn that all animals eat something, they all need to move, and they all must reproduce to preserve their species.

While doing these studies, the children are also learning to read or improve their reading skills. In our years of teaching, we have been amazed at how many students learned to read because of their interest in and enthusiastic use of these materials, particularly those focused on animals. Those who were still working with basic phonics and phonograms suddenly had a reason to translate that knowledge into the reading of labels. Those who already were emergent readers broadened their skills by working with the

Young students work with the classified cards in biology as part of the First Knowledge series of studies.

definitions, and the most advanced readers enjoyed challenging themselves with the definitions cut into strips and games that mixed up the lines.

We must, however, remind ourselves once again that it's not the biology terminology and content, or even the improvement of reading skills, that is the most important part of learning in the Montessori context of Cosmic Education. Rather, it's the mastery of an evolutionary pattern, an enrichment of the context the child can draw on to pursue his quest for an answer to the "Who am I?" question. Certainly, few children will think of that when they do this initial study, but they can use their knowledge of the pattern when they later meet the Timeline of Life and its story.

The Timeline of Life

Two students match loose pieces to the Timeline of Life charts. Strips along the top represent the various eras of life, while representative plants and animals are depicted on the black lines in the middle to show ancestral lineages.

A more advanced version of the Story of Life is told to the older children in the lower elementary class. A part of the timeline is turned into a linear clock representing the very last hours of the Clock of Eons, and more details are added for study with a Montessori material called the Timeline of Life. This is one of the major materials in the classroom, both in the amount of space it occupies and in the place of importance it holds in the curriculum. It also dominates an elementary classroom in the amount of work it takes for teachers to color and mount the pictorial panels of the timeline and in the amount of time it takes students to exhaust their interest in it. In our experience, this illustrated presentation of the Story of Life is most attractive to the oldest children in the six- to nine-year-old classroom, as a culminating activity following several years of preparatory work.

The Timeline of Life, with its heavy dependence on the evolutionary chain of events, gives Montessori students a framework in which to situate themselves in the whole process of unfolding life. From the earliest protein building blocks through the reign of the mammals, the children are able to trace the history of life on Earth, bringing their studies ever closer to their own place in the Universe. From the very end of the Proterozoic Era through the Neozoic Era, the child is exposed to the story of life, in pictures, as it evolved and developed on this planet of ours. Perhaps the story can be told an era at a time. For example:

> *The Paleozoic was the first major era of life on Earth. The name, taken from Greek, means "old life." During this time, life was mainly in the oceans, so we color this era blue for water. The era is divided into three ages: The Age of Invertebrates, the Age of Fish, and the Age of Amphibians. It is also divided into periods named after the places where main fossils have been found, such as Cambrian (for an area in Wales) and Devonian (for Devon, England).*
>
> *At the beginning of this era, the only life was microscopic. If we humans had been around at the time and decided to go swimming in the sea, we would have thought we were alone. The animals and plants were all tiny, with only one cell.*
>
> *As time went on, the Paleozoic Era brought an explosion of new types of animals, from invertebrates, to fish, to amphibians, with many different types of cells working together to make many different types of bodies. These animals built their bodies in special ways to solve problems and to make their lives easier. Here are some of the highlights pictured on our timeline from this era. . . .*[73]

In addition to the main story or Great Lesson contained in this account and others on the Mesozoic and Neozoic Eras, there are dozens of stories within

---

73 Quoted from the CMTE/NY history album used in the training course for teachers of 6–9-year-olds.

the story or "mini-lessons" which the teacher can offer the children. These include tales of the fascinating life forms pictured in this material—from the trilobites, those now-extinct, three-lobed creatures with many legs that lived in the muddy sea bottoms and which can be documented with real fossils in the classroom; through the dinosaurs, always a fascinating area of study for young children; up to the emergence of primates and humans. The ancient creatures pictured on the Timeline of Life can hold the same fascination for elementary children that dinosaurs alone hold for the younger child. An example of a mini-lesson on such creatures is one told in our training by Biff Maier, one of the best storytellers we know in Montessori:

> *Let me tell you about one of my favorite animals, the nautiloid. This animal builds a protective shell around itself, and when it outgrows the shell, it seals it all up, except for a small hole, and builds itself a bigger room to move into. This goes on until the nautiloid carries around a train of rooms, each bigger than the one before it, all connected only by the tube that goes through all the little holes. The nautiloid can move quickly by shooting water through the tube, like jet propulsion. Also, it can fill these empty rooms with water when it wants to sink deeper into the sea, or it can force the water out so that it rises higher in the water . . . like a submarine. Finally, it can shoot an inky liquid out to disguise its path and confuse enemies. This is a pretty inventive animal, to invent submarines (the first human-made sub was called Nautilus) and jets!*[74]

With such mini-lessons on a select few of the plants and animals depicted on the Timeline of Life, the children can be encouraged to meet even more of them through their own research in later study. Along the way, the children can be shown how plants and animals worked together, such as the giant ferns which fed the monstrous animals of the day and packed themselves into the ground to become our coal millions of years later.

In several chapters of *To Educate the Human Potential*, Maria Montessori herself develops many of the ideas for the Timeline of Life and gives us a series of stories about some of the main characters along the way. As she begins Chapter 4, she proclaims to us that "life is a cosmic agent,"[75] and she raises our consciousness of the role all creatures play in carrying out the

---

[74] Quoted from the CMTE/NY history album used in the training course for teachers of 6–9-year-olds.
[75] Maria Montessori, *To Educate,* p. 29.

cosmic plan. In Chapter 5, "The Drama of the Ocean," she speaks eloquently about such creatures as the trilobites, the cephalopods, the nautilus, the crinoids, the coral polyps, and other now extinct creatures that have come to be displayed on the Timeline of Life.

The crinoids, those animals that looked like tiny trees, are described in the context of the seas needing someplace to store their excess calcium and a committee of Angels going forth to look for volunteers.

> What a wonderful sight would have met their eyes when the Crinoids presented themselves! It was as if the bottom of the sea had become a forest of trees, with colorful branches waving like arms in the air, although there could have been no wind. We can imagine the Crinoids saying for themselves: "Look at us! We look like trees, but our trunks are made of stones among which we press our delicate bodies, so cementing them together as pillars; and we have branches, so that we can spread our arms to catch hold of the calcium that you want destroyed. It will serve us for food, and even when we die we shall not throw back the calcium, for we shall have consumed and transformed it."[76]

What makes Montessori's own words about these creatures so intriguing is not just the detailed and interesting story she provides in her discussion of each organism; most importantly, she never loses sight of the fact that each of them has a "cosmic task," a vital role to play in the unfolding of the Universe as it seeks to promote life. This is the real content of these studies, and this is what she emphasizes over and over.

As she explains her rationale:

> One side of evolution deals with the satisfaction of vital needs, defense, survival of the species and growth by modifications towards perfection. Another—and stronger—factor in evolutionary processes is concerned with the cosmic function of each living being, and even of inanimate natural objects, working in collaboration for the fulfillment of the Purpose of Life.[77]

---

76   Ibid., p. 36–37.

77   Ibid., p. 41.

Montessori teachers must take their cue from Maria Montessori herself. There's a remarkable foundation laid here for later scientific studies, an introduction to all the major terminology of evolutionary biology. Once again, however, it is not the details of the scientific content that are the point of all this work—it is the attempt to move closer to situating ourselves in the context of the whole. With the Timeline of Life, a new chapter of the story has been told, and the study has already begun.

The Timeline of Life is itself a major material for study on the part of the students. They can research some of the creatures depicted on the timeline, as mentioned above. They can expand their knowledge of the various eras on the timeline by studying the plants and animals depicted in each era. They can learn about the geological periods included in each of the eras. They can study the lines connecting various species of living creatures on the timeline and notice where they diverge to form a new kind of plant or animal, connecting this study with their work in classification or taxonomy. Finally, they can reconstruct the entire timeline using a mute or blank version of the panels and loose pieces that match the teacher-made timeline.

The Timeline of Life is a material that provides an opportunity for weeks or even months of study on the part of the students, with little guidance from the teacher beyond the telling of the story line.

Advanced Studies of Biology

In addition to the study of the Timeline of Life itself, there are other studies in biology that complement and expand on the historical presentation of this Great Lesson. Once again, our purpose is to situate them in the context of Cosmic Education:

1. First Classification

The biology study most directly related to the Timeline of Life is that of First Classification, in which students in Montessori lower elementary classes are introduced to the study of biological taxonomy, or the organization

Two boys compare the "mute" classification chart for prokaryotes and protoctista with the model chart to their left in First Classification studies.

of living creatures into categories according to their characteristics. The materials for this study are called First Classification since there is an Advanced Classification study for upper elementary students.

In the animal studies, if students have not already been introduced to the world of invertebrates, this material gives them a first taste. The classification charts consist of pictures of representative animals arranged in a pattern that moves from top to bottom and left to right. The left-to-right arrangement follows the evolutionary sequence, this time with invertebrates added to the sequence. The top-to-bottom arrangement goes from the level of *kingdom* (Animalia), to the various *phyla* of invertebrates vs. the vertebrate phylum, to the *class* level of Arthropoda and vertebrates, to the *order* level of insects and the *order* level of each vertebrate class.

This is an impressive collection of information. However, once again, we note that the primary purpose of these materials is not to infuse students with knowledge of biology to rival high school and even college students. The content students learn with this material is a useful byproduct of the process and a good foundation for work they will be doing in high school and beyond. However, the main purpose of the materials is to allow the children to really appreciate, through long-term exposure and study, the evolutionary pattern formed by the different characteristics of the animals portrayed on the classification charts.

Timeline of Life and First Classification are parallel studies, with the two reinforcing each other as history/biology mirror images. The more these two studies can be connected, the more effective they are for the students. Such an approach lays the groundwork for a better understanding of where we humans fit into the picture in attempting to answer the question "Who am I?"

There also are classification charts for plants which follow the same pattern of organization and present even more challenging information. Plant studies are always more difficult for young children than the more familiar animal studies. With the plant charts, students are exposed to such distinctions as those between vascular and non-vascular plants (those with tube-like organs for circulation and those without), between gymnosperms and angiosperms (naked seed plants and covered seeds), between monocotyledons and dicotyledons (single sprout and double sprout seeds). As with the animal kingdom, those distinctions can be traced on the Timeline of Life to reinforce the woven fabric of Cosmic Education.

In classrooms with updated materials, there are classification charts for the other three kingdoms of prokaryotes, protoctists, and fungi as well, with a similar purpose.

2. *Vital Functions*

The emphasis on biology in the Montessori curriculum which we have seen in the lower elementary classroom continues into the upper elementary level as well. There, older students revisit concepts they have already been exposed to in lower elementary, and they increase their knowledge with even more detailed, in-depth studies. The first example of this is the series of materials used for what is called the study of Vital Functions:[78] the vegetative functions of nutrition, respiration, and circulation; the relationship functions of the nervous and skeletal-muscular systems; and reproduction.

---

78 A lower elementary version of this used in some classrooms is called Body Functions, but it does not include invertebrates and is less detailed than Vital Functions.

This study would not be half so interesting if limited to the familiar vertebrates—most of the Vital Functions are very similar in all vertebrate classes. A comparison to the less familiar invertebrates provides some fascinating opportunities for understanding the miraculous processes that keep living organisms functioning and the remarkable complexity that evolution has produced in the diversity of life forms.

Things get even more complicated when the study moves to the Vital Functions of Plants. Plants have their own Vital Functions—they need the "vegetative" functions of nourishment, respiration, and circulation to survive; they have sensitivity to the outside environment, and they support themselves and "move" toward what they need; and they reproduce to maintain their species.

Since experiments can be done with plants in ways that would be inappropriate with animals, the Vital Functions of Plants study includes more than 20 experiments ranging from the observation of root growth patterns to tracing the path of plant circulation to demonstrations of such concepts as hydrotropism (movement toward water) and phototropism (movement toward light). There are also nearly as many charts, creatively produced by Mario Montessori and others, to illustrate important concepts along the way. Students learn about the nitrogen cycle, the chemistry of photosynthesis, and the complicated world of plant reproduction.

The content would challenge most high school students, and these are only 9- to 12-year-olds. However, the ideas are presented so concretely, through the experiments, that the knowledge is accessible and understandable. The students receive an amazingly rich foundation in biology.

The purpose is not to create walking encyclopedias of knowledge. The "stuff" the students learn is almost incidental to the enrichment of the context they gain for understanding themselves and their place in the Universe. Teachers should relate all the information students learn back to the story they heard with the Timeline of Life. We're still teaching for life, not for an achievement test. We're still dealing not only with biology, but with Cosmic Education, the search for our place in the Universe.

3. Advanced Classification

The final biology material that serves as an illustration/study of the Story of Life is the Advanced Classification work of the upper elementary. Building on the First Classification work done with the charts in lower elementary, students go into greater detail and depth in their studies of taxonomy.

First, a more scientific understanding is given of the various levels of classification, using a familiar animal as an example and a Russian nesting doll to keep track of the levels and give a sensorial experience of groups within groups. Hope, our dog, can be classified in the kingdom of Animalia; in the division of Chordata;[79] in the phylum of Vertebrata; in the class of Mammalia; in the order of Carnivora; in the family of Canidae; in the genus of *canis;* in the species of *Canis familiaris;* in the breed of German Shepherd; and with the individual name of Hope.

Then, the students are introduced to the "Chinese Box," a nesting doll series of levels of classification within levels of classification to illustrate the strata of the animal kingdom and the characteristics which distinguish each group of animals from others at the same level of classification. The materials include drawings to highlight the outstanding characteristics which distinguish each group. The study can proceed one level at a time, going deeper and deeper into the box as students learn phyla, classes, and orders of non-chordates and chordates. The materials usually end before they get to the level of family, genus, and species, but students can make their own connections by working backwards from their favorite species of animals. As a culminating activity which serves as a demonstration of knowledge, students create a "Tree of Life" for the animal kingdom, placing the same symbols used in the Chinese Box on the branches of a tree to give a final picture of the arrangement of the animal kingdom.

For the plant kingdom,[80] there are several options for Advanced Classification work. Schools can purchase materials similar to those for the animal kingdom from Montessori supply companies. They can acquire them through various training courses which have developed their own

---

79 Already in the Vital Function work, the students are introduced to the concept of chordata, or animals with a spinal cord to organize their nervous system. Transitional animals have notochords without the protection of a vertebral column of bone.

80 Comments about the plant kingdom also can be applied to the other three kingdoms—Prokaryotes, Protoctista, and Fungi—in classrooms that have adopted the five-kingdom system.

materials and have the trainees put them together for the classroom. Or, what might be the best course of action for the students, teachers can guide their class through the creation of their own materials based on the model of the animal kingdom. This last option is closer to the way Montessori probably envisioned this work, and it is a much more active process for the students, requiring real research and thinking about how to describe and illustrate the distinguishing characteristics.

What makes all this work interesting and useful is the foundation for talking about where humans fit into the picture, how the characteristics of *Homo sapiens* are similar and different from other organisms that have kept the Story of Life going on this planet for these billions of years.

Conclusion

As the sheer volume of this chapter demonstrates quite clearly, the Story of Life is really the heart and soul of the Montessori cultural curriculum. This may be because of the children's innate fascination with these studies, the developmentally appropriate nature of animal studies, or because of Maria Montessori's own background in medicine. Whatever the reason, the Story of Life, in both the telling of the story and in the numerous biology studies that go along with it, dominates the Montessori cultural curriculum and the shelves of a Montessori classroom.

Montessori teachers who lose sight of the guiding principles of Cosmic Education can easily become obsessed with making sure their students know every little fact and detail of the story and the biology studies outlined above. Doing so would be a mistake that could diminish the whole learning experience for the children in their charge. To insist on memorization of details or regurgitation of facts would likely deaden students' sense of awe and excitement over the diversity of life on our planet. It would lessen their chances of seeing the all-important patterns formed by life's myriad species, and would impede the children from recognizing their cosmic position in this array of organisms. The guiding questions remain: "Who am I? Where do I come from? Why am I here?"

Chapter 8

The Story of Humans

THE NEXT CONCENTRIC CIRCLE draws us into the realm of our own species, into the world of humans, into the very origins of *Homo sapiens.* The study of history now takes on a new interest and relevance for children. Now, the object of that study is their own family, their own particular place in the wealth of living species on the Earth.

Traditional education spends little time on so-called pre-history, the time of human existence before the relatively late invention of writing. What a shame! There are more than two million years of human history by the reckoning of most archeologists today, yet some educators limit themselves to studying the last 5,000 years or so of that history. Montessori begins long before that period.

This is an area where we meet another of Montessori's original Great Lessons, the Story of Humans. Her curriculum has an entire sequence of presentations on the emergence of early humans that many Montessori schools reserve for their upper elementary classes. A parallel study of human biology is also usually presented in the upper elementary level.

This is where the "Who am I?" question begins to take on a more personal tone, where the context of study narrows to the human species itself.

The Story of Early Humans

The Montessori curriculum takes great pains to search out our early ancestors, to delve into their way of life and to give students an appreciation for all that they have inherited from these distant ancestors. This avoids the arrogance of focusing exclusively on Western civilization; in fact, the bulk of the study is not even on civilization itself. The human story, or "history," begins long before the invention of writing. The Montessori curriculum brings the child back to the stories of his or her most ancient human ancestors, deep into the period others call prehistoric—from *Homo habilis,* to *Homo erectus,* to *Homo sapiens* as Neanderthal and Cro-Magnon.[81]

Before the actual story is told, the students do preliminary research to find the species that are their closest *living* relatives, using the knowledge they acquired in classification studies connected with the Story of Life. The students are led through a taxonomic examination of *Homo sapiens*—helping them understand why they are considered part of the vertebrate phylum of animals, the class of mammals, the order of primates, and the family of apes. They can feel their own backbones and know they belong with the vertebrates. They know from their own family experience that humans have live babies instead of laying eggs, and that they nurse their young like other mammals. They examine themselves for the critical characteristics linking them to primates and apes—shorter canine teeth, stereoscopic vision, fingers and toenails instead of claws. One exercise that always catches the fascination of the students is to have them spend a day with their thumb taped to their hand, demonstrating in dramatic fashion the importance of the opposable thumb to humans and other primates.

After a thorough examination of comparative characteristics in bones, teeth, soft body parts, and even chromosomes, they eventually narrow the search for our closest living relative to the gorilla or the chimpanzee. One class of students in our school spent several weeks doing research in encyclopedias, biology books, magazines, and on the Internet to try to resolve the argument of which was closest (we eventually declared it a tie from the evidence we found in our research).

---

81 *Homo habilis* (handy man), *Homo erectus* (upright human), and *Homo sapiens* (wise human) are generally accepted within the scientific community as the principal human species or stages in the development of humans. However, the picture is much more complicated than that, and new evidence of human species or sub-species is constantly being uncovered.

To prepare the way for a search for our closest *extinct* relatives and to set up the actual story, the students are introduced to some basic techniques of archeology. We usually create a simulated dump site in a trash can and layer artifacts to represent the technological progress of successive generations of humans from the earliest stone age to our plastic-dumping contemporaries. Then we do an impressionistic dig in which students play a variety of roles on the archeology team to uncover the artifacts. On our school property, we are fortunate to have an old farm site and students have done actual archeological digs to uncover artifacts from the past, including roof slates, parts of metal tools like hand plows and scythes, square nails that look like they could have been made by a blacksmith, and bottles with old inscriptions — all clues to life more than one hundred years ago.

In the classroom, students examine a stretched-out, four-meter-long version of the thin red strip at the end of the Timeline of Life and discover the telling characteristic of toolmaking represented by a hand holding a stone halfway through the strip. The real surprise comes at the end as they find a tiny golden strip, barely a half centimeter wide, representing the time of human writing and written history. This is an impressionistic lesson similar to the Long Black Line, allowing for an initial telling of the Story of Humans in condensed form. Another version of this story could be told with the help of Morgan's third book in her trilogy, *Mammals Who Morph: The Universe Tells Our Evolution Story* (Dawn Publications, 2006). With this background, the students are ready to explore the past in a search for relatives in the time of the first humans.

The students examine the fossil record for these ancient relatives, beginning with such extinct hominids as *Ramapithecus* and *Australopithecus*.[82] Archeologists have uncovered only jawbones from *Ramapithecus*, but even that limited evidence shows a short muzzle that puts them closer to humans than the gorillas and chimps of today. The more complete skeletons of *Australopithecus*, including the famous 3.5 million-year-old "Lucy" skeleton discovered in 1974 in Ethiopia, shows evidence of bipedalism. That trait puts them closer to humans than gorillas and chimps, who can walk on two legs but generally walk by balancing on their knuckles instead. The story of

---

82 These are both hominids, or human-like creatures. The root word "pithecus" comes from the Greek word for ape, while "Rama" refers to an Indian god. We find pithecus again in *Australopithecus*, with "australo" deriving from the Greek word for southern.

how "Lucy" was found and named makes a fascinating tale for the students along the way.[83]

The first real "human," *Homo habilis*, is the next character in the story. This toolmaking creature, "Handyman," has a shortened muzzle, bipedal skeleton, an enlarged brain, and an association with primitive stone tools. These are the first fossils we classify in the genus *Homo*, or human, although they are still distinct enough to be called a separate species from ourselves.

Maria Montessori, in Chapter 10 of *To Educate the Human Potential*, talks about Early Man and the significance of those crude stone tools left behind as evidence of the presence of humans. "Significant it is that man should leave behind him his handiwork, traces of his creative intelligence, instead of his bodily remains among those of the lesser animals. Here is the colossal difference in this new cosmic energy."[84]

The real Story of Humans begins to be told with the emergence of tools — created by hands left free in a being who can now walk on two legs. This, finally, is an animal we recognize as one like us. The story of these first humans might be told somewhat like the following:[85]

> *Habilines lived in East Africa from about two and a half million years ago to about one million years ago. . . . These earliest of humans had to stay where it was warm because they wore no clothes and they had not learned how to use fire.*
>
> *Habilines lived in open country. They preferred to camp beside lakes . . . they built shelters out of branches that were held in place with stones. One of the important differences between these first humans and apes was the use of a home base. Habilines hunted and gathered during the day, but they carried food back to their camp at night.*
>
> *. . . When habilines hunted, they had only the weapons that they found around them. They picked up stones to hit or throw at animals, and they stabbed at their prey with pointed sticks. With simple weapons like these,*

---

83   Donald Johanson and Maitland Edey, *Lucy — the Beginnings of Humankind*. The account of the finding and naming of Lucy is in the prologue.

84   Maria Montessori, *To Educate*, p. 65.

85   The story elements in this chapter are excerpts from the CMTE/NY history albums for the 9 to 12 training course.

they were probably not very successful hunters, able to kill only small mammals when they had the opportunity.

. . . As far as we know, habilines were the first animals to deliberately make and use stone tools. They learned to hold a stone in one hand and to strike it with another stone in order to knock flakes off. This became a sharp chopping tool . . . to smash the bones and skulls of animals so they could eat the brains and marrow.

Next comes *Homo erectus* who, in addition to all the human characteristics of *Homo habilis,* is found to have been associated with the use of fire. The domestication of fire put these physically puny humans at a distinct advantage over other species of animals. They no longer had to depend solely on what nature offered them for light and warmth. They could use fire to cook their food, particularly those hard-to-chew chunks of meat. They could use fire as a tool to defend themselves against predators and enhance their success in a hunt for their own prey. Harnessing the energy of fire was the beginning of the human domination of the planet.

By about a million years ago, a new type of human was living in Africa. Groups of these new "upright humans" hunted animals in Africa, Asia and Europe until about 200,000 years ago.

. . . Upright humans probably lived together in small groups. They may have taken specialized jobs: some gathering plants and small animals, some hunting large game, some caring for the young. These people may have been the first to create a human language.

About a million years ago, upright humans began making a new kind of tool. It was shaped like a pear, with two sharp edges . . . we call these tools handaxes. . . . A habiline chopper could be made by knocking about 10 flakes off a lump of stone. **Homo erectus** *toolmakers removed from 100 to 200 flakes to make a handaxe.*

. . . It seems that **Homo erectus** *was the first to learn to use and control fire. Since all animals except humans are afraid of fire, early humans could use fire to protect themselves . . . the heat of fire may have made*

it possible for these early humans to move out of Africa and into cooler lands in Asia and Europe. It is interesting to guess how Homo erectus *first began to use the fire to cook food. Did a piece of meat happen to fall into the flames? Did hungry hunters try eating the meat of an animal who had perished in a grass fire? Some raw foods were impossible for humans to eat, but cooking allowed* Homo erectus *to eat more things. The cooked food was more tender, so chewing became easier. Over the years, as humans chewed less, the shape of their faces changed. The teeth became smaller, so the jaw or mouth no longer stuck out as far.*

The next character in the Story of Early Humans is our own species, *Homo sapiens,* first in the Neanderthal version and later in the Cro-Magnon variety leading right up to modern humans.[86] Neanderthals introduced the novelty of burying their dead, indicating some belief in a spirit life and survival after death. Cro-Magnons brought us the glories of cave paintings and other forms of art, the first symbolic expression which would eventually lead into what we consider writing.

> *About 250,000 years ago, people with brains as large as our own appeared. These new people are called "*Homo sapiens,*" or "wise humans." . . . For the last 150,000 years,* Homo sapiens *has been the only species of humans on Earth. . . .*[87]

> *The Neanderthals used the skins of animals to clothe themselves. Humans became the only warm-blooded creatures that kill other animals and wrap themselves in their skins to keep warm.*

> *. . . Unlike any animals before them, "wise humans" buried their dead. Instead of burying in a far-away cemetery, they dug graves in the floors of their huts and caves. It seems that they believed that the person's spirit continued to live after death, so they wanted to keep them at home.*

---

86 Neanderthal and Cro-Magnon are considered to be the same species, *Homo sapiens,* despite their considerable physical differences. Scientists are divided over whether Neanderthals were bred out of existence as a sub-species through mingling with Cro-Magnons or whether they were killed off by their fellow *Homo sapiens.*

87 In contrast to the unity of human species in modern times, paleoanthropologists like Ian Tattersall of the Museum of Natural History in New York stress the contemporary co-existence of several species of humans in the more distant past. See his book, *The Human Odyssey,* New York, Prentice Hall, 1993.

. . . Sometime between 40,000 and 30,000 years ago, modern people began to appear in Europe. These people are often called "Cro-Magnon" people after the rock shelter in France where remains of this type were found.

A student lays out the "parade of hominids" to show the developing human characteristics that lead to Homo sapiens *in Early Human studies.*

. . . Cro-Magnon people did something no earlier humans had done. They created works of art. They made paintings on rocks and caves. They made sculptures out of stone, ivory, bone, and clay. They carved designs on rocks, bones, and antlers. Finally, they made ornaments to decorate their bodies.

This "parade of the hominids" leads right up to our own species and offers an opportunity for a philosophical discussion of how humans are similar to but different from other species of animals. It allows the young students to see themselves as belonging to one species out of many species, and yet—at the same time—to see their history rooted in the emergence of this highly developed species that has come to dominate our planet.

Christian, in his course on Big History, advances the theory that what sets humans apart is not tool making—chimpanzees have been observed making tools to extract termites from mounds, for example. He says that our use of symbolic language allows us to adapt to our environment in a unique way involving "collective learning."

All living species succeed or fail based on their ability to adapt to their environment, and collective learning gives humans a qualitatively different way of adapting that allows them to constantly find new ways to extract energy from the environment and ensure their survival. As a historian, Christian sees collective learning, or the ability to exchange large amounts of learned information, as the emergent characteristic that allows humans alone to have a "history."

That history, in a Montessori context, is contained in one of the Great Lessons of Cosmic Education. Story, study, and timeline merge in a single material called the Timeline of Early Humans. Although the dates change slightly as new archeological evidence is unearthed, the timeline is measured in successive ages marking human advances, from the use of tools, to the harnessing of fire, to the development of burial rituals acknowledging the spiritual side of human life, to the expression of that spirit in the artistic creations of cave paintings, statues, pottery, and jewelry.

The Story of Modern Humans

Story, study, and timeline are extended into the time of "modern humans" from the Stone Age periods of the Upper Paleolithic and Mesolithic.[88] Remains of those human groups of nomadic hunter/gatherers have been found mostly throughout Europe. Paleolithic cultures in the continuing story include the Aurignacians, who lived in modern-day France and decorated the insides of caves with colorful paintings of the animals they hunted; Gravettians, who lived in eastern Europe, learned how to construct man-made houses, and left behind intriguing statuettes of buxom female figures called "Venuses"; Solutreans, who lived in France after the Aurignacians and who are believed to have invented such technological advances as laurel leaf-shaped spear points and needles with an eye for threading; and Magdalenians, from southwest France and northern Spain, who used high-tech stone age tools like the first harpoons and the atlatl spear-thrower.

From the Mesolithic period, students study the Azilians, who lived in the forests of Europe and invented the bow and arrow, with fine points called microliths; Maglemosians, who lived in the swampy bogs of northern Europe and who invented the first true axe with a handle and are thought

---

88   The "Upper Paleolithic" is an archeological term, with "upper" signifying "most recent" in the strata of a dig, "paleo" meaning""old," and""lithic" coming from the Greek word for "stone." Mesolithic means "middle stone age."

THE STORY OF HUMANS 109

to have been the first people to adopt dogs as pets and helpers; and Kitchen Midden Folk, who lived in present-day Denmark and who left behind huge mounds of shells from oysters and other shellfish.[89]

Finally, we come to the Neolithic[90] period where we meet those amazing peoples who invented agriculture, both in the herding of animals and the planting of crops, pottery, weaving, and all the other wonders that made village life possible and vaulted humans into a new age of existence. Students learn about the organization of village life, and they become familiar with the people who built those megalithic monuments found from Mediterranean islands to Stonehenge in the British Isles.

Swimme and Berry, in *The Universe Story,* dedicate an entire chapter of their book to the significance of the Neolithic culture. Among other interesting theories they explore is one suggesting that women were primarily responsible for the major advances of society in farming, weaving, and pottery, and that the people of this time viewed the deity as a goddess rather than a male figure. They vividly describe Neolithic villages, such as Jericho in Palestine, Jarmo and Hassuna on the upper Tigris River, and Catal Huyuk in central Anatolia.[91] They argue that the eventual passage from the Neolithic village to urban centers caused such damage to the planet that humanity may be forced to return to the village model to rescue the planet from destruction.[92]

Finally, having explored the societal changes of the Neolithic villages, the students are led through a study of humans in the Age of Metals—first as the Bronze Age, and then the Iron Age. The idea of combining mineral ores of copper and tin from the earth to make bronze revolutionized the way humans could make their tools and weapons, showing a level of intellect and creativity as yet unseen on this planet. Iron, however, was more abundant and was to dominate technology through the industrial revolution of the 19th century. As long as 4,500 years ago, the peoples of Asia Minor were hammering iron from meteorites into ornaments and ceremonial weapons.

---

89 The peoples studied in this section were all found in Europe. This concentration is partially a cultural bias, but it is also due to the more extensive archeological evidence uncovered in this area of the world.

90 Neolithic means "new stone age."

91 Swimme and Berry, *The Universe Story,* p. 166–170.

92 Ibid., p. 179.

Within the next thousand years, the dominance of iron ushered in the modern age.

This study of two million years of the human story brings students into the time of what we call history—or written history. It also gives them all the elements they need to create a wonderful timeline stretching from the appearance of the first hominids up to the time of recorded history.

Maria Montessori recognized the significance of the advances made by these early humans. "*Homo sapiens* had arrived and . . . he was able to cultivate the richly fertile soil, domesticating animals to serve him and keeping dogs to guard them. He was master of all, dressing in skins or woven cloth from sheep's wool, with bow and arrows for weapons as well as knives, using ornaments of jade, gold, and bronze, and artistic pottery for domestic purposes. This was an advanced civilization. . . ."[93]

This study of "prehistoric" humans is an impressive body of study, delving into areas that most students never become familiar with unless they study anthropology in college. Even high school students in the United States have only fleeting exposure to the existence of prehistoric humans, and they certainly don't spend much time or learn many details about these ancient ancestors. Yet, all this is offered to elementary-aged children as a normal and very important part of the Montessori curriculum.

Why? These lessons are all part of the Cosmic Education curriculum, an attempt to help children better understand who they are by learning where they come from and who their ancestors were. How can we understand our own story, our place in the bigger Story of the Universe, if we leave out this all-important chapter of how we got here? How can we make sense of the last 5,000 years of our "history" if we leave out the more than two million years of so-called "prehistory" of humans on this planet?

This perspective allows us to compare humans with other species of animals and to see how we are different, something Maria Montessori did so eloquently in *To Educate the Human Potential:*

> Man is relatively of little strength, with naked skin, weaponless and at a disadvantage physically to many other mammals, but he is given intelligence in rich measure, because he is destined to accomplish an essential work of creation, more than any other expression of life that has evolved. His new weapon was the mental one. . . .

[93] Maria Montessori, *To Educate*, p. 70.

Man is God's chief agent on earth for creation, not come merely to be its lord and enjoy himself, to be proud and boast as do the foolish. . . . The truly great are humble! But we may legitimately be proud and rejoice that man has transformed his world in the long course of ages to one that is now beyond nature's contriving. Finding conditions worse when he came than any imagined for a Robinson Crusoe, man has built civilization.[94]

It is this perspective of humanity's comparison to other species which is important for the Montessori student. It is this step toward understanding who we are and where we come from that makes this study worthwhile.

Human Biology

The principal study connected with the Story of Humans is included in the creation of the Timeline of Humans, as outlined above. However, just as there are parallel studies in biology to accompany the Timeline of Life, there are studies in human biology that complement the Timeline of Humans. Because the focus is now on humans themselves, detailed studies of human anatomy and physiology are appropriate subjects of study. Once again, the Montessori curriculum in this area is generally reserved for detailed study at the upper elementary level.

There is an impressionistic chart and presentation called The Great River to introduce this study. Comparing the human organism to a great river of blood and blood vessels, the chart is topped by a castle representing the Department of the President, or the controlling influence of the brain. In the center of the chart is the Department of Transportation, representing the circulatory pump of the heart; there are Departments of Respiration and Nutrition, Defense (the immune system), Purification (kidneys and bowels), and Reproduction.

This leads into a study of the human body as an organism made up of systems, organs, tissues, and cells. In presenting the cell, we have had a lot of success in constructing a model of the cell in a large glass container filled with light red Jell-o, with items representing the parts of the cell dispersed throughout the gelatin (cytoplasm), such as the nucleus and the mitochon-

---

94   Maria Montessori, *To Educate*, p. 66–67.

dria. As we give the names of the parts and explain their function, we dig the items out of the Jell-o one at a time with gloved hands plunged into the messy mixture, much to the delight of the students. After the parts of the cell are studied, the various types of human cells are introduced to see how they each do a different kind of job—blood, muscle, bone, nerve, and skin. All this leads to a study of human body systems which represent the human version of the Vital Functions study for other living organisms.[95]

The function of movement brings attention to the human skeleton and muscles, with students going as far as their interest will carry them in learning the names and functions of the bones and muscles of the body. The various types of joints in the body can also be learned. An interesting experiment to show the bones' need for calcium is to place a chicken bone in a beaker of vinegar or diluted hydrochloric acid. After a few days, the bone becomes rubbery as the calcium is dissolved, and the remaining cartilage can even be tied in a knot. A friendly butcher can cut cross sections in a large animal bone to show the construction of the outer covering, the spongy inside, and the marrow.

With nutrition, the entire process of human digestion can be studied, including the physical and chemical breakdown that begins in the mouth, the digestive juices poured into the stomach and intestines, the process of chemical transformation and absorption of the various nutrients, and ending with the excretory functions. The whole process is filled with delicate balances of chemistry that can produce real awe in the students and an appreciation of the fragile nature of the process.

For experiments connected with this study, the children can test various foods to see if they are protein, starch, or fat. Tincture of iodine turns blue-black in the presence of starch, fatty foods will make brown paper squares translucent when rubbed on them, and a solution of potassium hydroxide plus a few drops of diluted copper sulfate will turn pink or bluish in the presence of protein.[96] If you live in a rural area, you may be able to convince a local farmer to provide body parts such as a cow or pig stomach for class-

---

[95] There is a good multimedia supplement to these studies in the CD-ROM *A.D.A.M., The Inside Story*, put out by A.D.A.M. Software Inc. of Atlanta in 1994. The material is presented in a clever, attractive, and understandable way without sacrificing scientific accuracy or detail.

[96] This and some other examples of activities in this chapter are taken from a great little book by Linda Allison, *Blood and Guts: A Working Guide to Your Own Insides*. Boston: Little, Brown and Company 1976.

room examination; or, in the city, you could approach a butcher or meat packer.

The function of respiration touches on the chemical exchanges of oxygen and carbon dioxide which take place in the lungs and within each cell of the body. The function of circulation involves a detailed study of the heart and the various blood vessels of the body as they bring life-preserving nutrients and oxygen to each cell and take away waste products which could poison the body if not removed.

A homemade stethoscope can be made from rubber tubing and a plastic funnel purchased at the hardware store so students can hear their heartbeats. To give an idea of how hard the heart works to pump blood through the body, have students squeeze a tennis ball about 70 times a minute. For the truly ambitious, a dissected cow's heart can be examined to display valves and chambers dramatically.

The function of sensing the outside environment leads to an examination of the entire nervous system, from brain to spinal column to nerve endings for the various senses of the human body. The study can extend to the way nerves transmit their messages between the brain and the organs which gather information from sight, hearing, smell, taste, and touch. Student interest in these areas will often push the teacher to expand his or her own knowledge of human anatomy and physiology.

The brain of a cow (from that friendly farmer or meat packer) can give the children an idea of how brain tissue looks. Reaction time, or the time it takes to send a message to the brain and elicit a response, can be tested by having one student drop a ruler between the extended thumb and index finger of a classmate to see if it can be caught before it slips through. Students also can do dominance tests of their hands, feet, eyes, and ears.

Finally, the reproductive function is studied in humans, allowing a range of presentations from a simple outline of the anatomy of human sex organs and cells to a complete sex education program appropriate to the ages of the children in the class. We have found that both parents and students are enthusiastic about a program offering information about sexual reproduction and associated issues within the context of a year-long study of the human body.[97]

---

[97] The same people who put out the CD-ROM on human biology cited above, A.D.A.M. Software Inc., produced another one in 1995 called *Nine Month Miracle,* which is a beautiful study of the development of the fetus and embryo during pregnancy.

The children's fascination with their own bodies is evident long before we reach the part about sex education. There are few subjects which have more natural attraction to students than those on human biology, and these studies present a wonderful opportunity to build within themselves a sense of deep appreciation for the delicate balances that keep their body functioning in good health. They will marvel over the trace chemicals necessary for human life and the way human body systems interact so delicately with each other. They will know themselves better by knowing how their bodies function, and perhaps they will be inspired to care for their bodies by eating a balanced diet, exercising properly, getting fresh air and sufficient rest, and not smoking or taking drugs.

The wonder of the human body, in all its delicate balancing acts, mirrors the wonder students first felt when they learned that the Universe itself is kept in existence by a balance of forces, gravitation operating against forces that pull things apart. From the unfolding of the Universe to the functioning of the human body, there is a need for understanding that produces awe within the conscious, reflective, thinking human spirit. Cosmic Education can nurture this special understanding.

Conclusion

As the child searches for an answer to the questions "Who am I? Where do I come from? Why am I here?," he moves from Universe, to solar system, to Earth, to the evolution of life and to the emergence of the human—a critical point in his self-understanding. If these lessons are presented without the arrogant boasting that often infects the study of the human, they bring the child closer to an understanding of his or her special place in the evolutionary chain.

The unique task of humans is to enable the Universe to reflect upon itself. They are not meant to dominate and exploit the rest of creation without regard to their kinship with other living organisms, indeed with the entire inanimate world. As children understand this relationship, they are less likely to disregard or disrespect this sacred connection.

With the story of humans placed in its proper context, children can more consciously begin to define the cosmic role their species has played and will continue to play in the Universe.

As Mario Montessori, Jr. put it in *Education for Human Development*:

> Children at this stage are fascinated because this story concerns them personally. They are beginning to be aware of their own situation as developing human beings. It also makes them conscious in a natural way of the difference between man and other living beings. There is an interrelationship between both and the environment. This interrelationship is evident in what Maria Montessori referred to as the cosmic task—the service that must be rendered by individuals of each species to the environment on which they are dependent for their existence to maintain it in such a way that it will support their descendants, generation after generation.[98]

---

98 Mario Montessori, Jr., *Education*, p. 104.

The Story of the Universe

The Story of the Stars and the Solar System

The Story of the Earth

The Story of Life

The Story of Humans

The Story of Civilization

History

Archaeology

Biology

Geology & Geography

Physics & Chemistry

Metaphysics & Astronomy

Chapter 9

The Story of Civilizations

ONCE THE CHILDREN HAVE been brought to this point of understanding about themselves, to the context which forms the backdrop of their lives, they can step inside the final concentric circle and sample what we have traditionally called history—the study of the Great Civilizations, leading up to and through the study of their own nation. Finally, we have reached the time of written history. Here, most observers would say, the Montessori curriculum matches the traditional curriculum of elementary students throughout the Western world.

However, that would be true only in regard to the time period covered, since the content of Montessori's presentation of history is not what we usually find in textbooks. It is not primarily focused on rulers and wars, on the dates and events which constitute the typical textbook curriculum. Montessori was much more concerned with the development of ideas and the pioneering discoveries that have allowed humans to move forward. She emphasized the daily lifestyle of the common people over a recitation of the exploits of the leaders in each civilization.

Montessori and History

Maria Montessori gives her views on classical history in a series of chapters in *To Educate the Human Potential*. She first engages in a rather philosophical discussion in a chapter entitled "Man the Creator and Revealer." Only then does she move to a discussion in later chapters of the ancient civilizations of India, China, Egypt, Mesopotamia, Greece, and Rome.

In that first, more philosophical chapter, Montessori describes history as a study of human striving and the discovery of new modes of living in the face of challenge and adversity. History is an account of the forward motion of humanity, a kind of timeline of pioneers who bring progress to humanity through technological advances that open unexplored frontiers for the human mind. "We must ourselves feel—and inspire in the children—admiration for all pioneers, known and unknown, possessors of the flame which has lighted the path of humanity."[99]

She notes that most people go through life with little interest in the progress of humanity, wanting merely to enjoy life. It is only the truly adventurous who are willing to forgo their own comfort and even risk their lives to bring about real change.

> We do not cultivate admiration for these past and present adventurers and explorers for the sake of paying them with our gratitude, for they are beyond our reach; but we want to help the child to realize the part that humanity has played and still has to play, because such realization leads to an uplift of soul and conscience. History must be alive and dynamic, awaking enthusiasm, destruction of intellectual egoism and selfish sloth . . . the history of human achievements is real, a living witness to the greatness of man, and the children can easily be brought to thrill to the knowledge that there are millions of people like themselves, striving mentally and physically to solve the problems of life, and that all contribute to a solution, though one may find it.[100]

Montessori goes on to explain that, although great discoveries are usually attributed to a single person, their contributions are the "crys-

---

99 Maria Montessori, *To Educate*, p. 77.

100 Ibid., p. 80–81.

tallization point of hundreds of intellects," and they stand on the shoulders of those who have gone before them: "The present stands on the past, as a house on its foundation."[101]

Finally, she talks about human history as the continuation of creation, man's acceptance of his role—cosmic task—of continuing the divine creation.

> Man has gone far beyond nature in the work of creation, and he could not have done so unless he had accepted and felt a God with no hands or feet, who yet walks through the length and breadth of the Universe, fashioned and still being wrought by Him, through human and other agents.[102]

Montessori puts herself firmly in the camp of those who see human history as a continuation of creation, and this shapes her view of the task of education. History must be taught, she insists, within the broader context of Cosmic Education.

FUNDAMENTAL HUMAN NEEDS

History is the telling of a story. There is an initial exploration of the Story of Civilizations at the lower elementary level, where the children are given a series of lessons and presentations called the Fundamental Needs of Humans.[103] Already from their first year in the elementary level, the children are taught about the common characteristics of human society from Stone Age peoples all the way to their own contemporary place in time. This version of the story includes its own timeline and study as well.

To illustrate the place of these fundamental human needs, Montessori tells the story of the Greek historian Herodotus, who traveled the known world for 17 years to see for himself how people lived outside Greece. Asked on his return if he had seen a Cyclops, centaurs, or mermaids, "he answered that he had seen not these but greater wonders, men much like himself

---

101 Ibid., p. 81.

102 Ibid., p. 82.

103 This was originally called the Fundamental Needs of Man. Montessori lived in a time when language was still dominated by masculine forms of expression.

Two girls place cards for housing and clothing on a timeline as part of their Fundamental Human Needs studies.

in all countries, eating and sleeping and dressing much as he did."[104]

Montessori was impressed by the fact that, although humans have made remarkable progress throughout history, they are simply changing the way they meet the universal, constant needs of all humans throughout time and space. Those needs are identical for people who live in different places throughout our globe, and they are the same for people who have lived from the time of the Stone Age until the present. This is what she wants teachers to impress on the children.

The children start this work with a discussion of what they would do if they were stranded on an island and had to figure out what they needed to survive. If we can convince them that they can survive without video games, they soon come to the fundamental needs of all humans: the material needs of nourishment, clothing, shelter, defense, and transportation; and the spiritual needs of art, religion, and self-adornment. There is a classic Montessori chart illustrating these fundamental needs. A second chart detailing the need of nutrition provides a model for further study of all types of needs and graphically illustrates the dependence of humans on the plant, animal, and mineral world for survival.

The students are then led through a series of "vertical" and "horizontal" studies of specific examples showing how those needs are met. The vertical

---

104 Maria Montessori, *To Educate*, p. 78.

studies mimic an archeological dig and take a single need, such as nourishment or transportation, and trace it throughout history as the dig reaches deeper and older layers. The horizontal studies focus on all the elements of a single civilization found within a single layer of the archeological dig.

As an example of a vertical study, the teacher can present an impressionistic lesson on the history of light, beginning with the simple fires of prehistoric peoples. A stick wrapped in chicken fat effectively illustrates the portable fire of a torch in a way that impresses the students. Then, candles and Grecian-style oil lamps show how ancient civilizations created their light. An antique kerosene lamp and a camping gas lantern are examples of a further development of the idea of a portable and adjustable light source. Finally, an electric light bulb, a flashlight, and a fluorescent light in the classroom complete the journey through time to the present.

These items are then placed on a timeline of civilizations beginning with prehistoric humans and usually including representative (Western) civilizations throughout history such as the Egyptians, the Greeks, Europeans in the Middle Ages, during the Renaissance, and in Modern Times. There are card materials with pictures, labels, and stories of housing, clothing, means of defense, transportation, religious beliefs, and other fundamental needs which can be matched vertically, one set at a time, to the stages of civilization.

In the context of a lesson entitled Fundamental Needs of Humans, it is somewhat surprising to find a material so Eurocentric as this in the standard Montessori repertoire. This material could be made much more interesting and effective in teaching the fundamental unity of humankind within the diversity of time and place if it included other ancient civilizations, such as those of India and China, or even the Mayan, Aborigine, and Inuit. Teachers can either create these materials themselves, or they can lead the children through research to produce appropriate illustrations and place them on the timeline.

The same materials laid out for the vertical studies—whether the usual ones or a more inclusive version—can then be used for horizontal studies of each civilization, allowing the children to develop in detail the look and feel of a particular period of history. Instead of using the cards representing one set of needs at a time, the child finds all the cards matching a single civilization—e.g., Egyptian—and creates a horizontal layout of their clothing, houses, transportation, defense, religion, art, and all the rest. This provides the framework and basic information for a report on a single civilization.

The recognition that people in very different places in the world, and in very ancient times, all had the same needs that we have today is a deeply spiritual insight for children on the fundamental unity of all human beings. This is Cosmic Education at the level of history, a presentation of history that is not at all like the one we typically find in elementary school textbooks. This is teaching history the way Montessori envisioned it for children.

THE GREAT CIVILIZATIONS

The upper elementary study of the Great Civilizations plays off the common human characteristics already covered by the younger children in their study of Fundamental Needs. Whether focusing on the ancient civilizations of China, India, Mesopotamia, and Egypt or the foundations of Western civilization in Rome and Greece, or the "New World" civilizations of the Aztecs, Incas, and Mayas, the Montessori study of World History does not limit itself to the ebb and flow of macro-events of wars and succession of rulers to tell the human story. There is just as much emphasis on the everyday lives of the people of these great civilizations and the legacy they left us from their collective wisdom.[105]

Maria Montessori begins her discussion of these ancient civilizations by recognizing the antiquity of the eastern civilizations of China and India, an idea still new in her day. "Civilization had of late been regarded as mostly a western product, linked only slightly with ancestral centers in the east. . . . Asiatic civilizations of advanced type far antedate European, and even Egyptian. . . . "[106]

Her special affinity for India, where she published her book *To Educate the Human Potential*, comes through clearly. "India became a great link between

---

[105] A wonderful supplementary resource for use in the classroom that dwells on some of these same everyday aspects is a series of videos called "Ancient Civilizations for Children" produced by Schlessinger Media. Included in the series are videos on ancient civilizations of China, Egypt, Mesopotamia, the Aegean, Africa, Greece, Rome, Inca, and Maya.

[106] Maria Montessori, *To Educate*, p. 83–84.

the most ancient and later civilizations, making a somewhat uneasy whole through some irreconcilable differences, but developing rare tolerance and cohesive social structure through its great leaders, philosophers and saints."[107] She shows great admiration for Indian thinkers and religious figures.

Next, she talks about the contributions of the Chinese to civilization, from the wisdom of Confucius to the art of printing. Students are usually fascinated by ancient Chinese civilization, which brought such innovations as papermaking and fireworks under dynasties that ruled for millennia.

Each of these studies must be accompanied by student activities. A survey of the Indian deities provides an opportunity for some interesting storytelling with the help of the appropriate resources.[108] We were fortunate in our school to have a family from India who shared the customs of their ancient civilization with the class. As for ancient China, the discovery of paper can be an opportunity for a papermaking project in the class.

Montessori devotes an entire chapter of her book to ancient Egypt, that central link between East and West, the thousands of years-old civilization that brought together the inventions of the past and offered its own discoveries for the future of the Western world. Children never cease to be fascinated with the pyramids, the embalming process and mummies, new methods of irrigation, the Pharaohs, Egyptian gods and goddesses, art, and jewelry. We have usually simulated the embalming process in the classroom during this study, with one student being appropriately wrapped as a mummy. There is a rich lore of Egyptian study documented in every major history museum in the world. We highly recommend a field trip to such a museum, if at all possible.

Some Montessori classrooms have consolidated the entire study of civilizations to an in-depth examination of the Egyptian city of Alexandria. Opting for depth rather than breadth, for detail rather than broad strokes, some teachers have found that a study of Alexandria can provide a prototype of civilization that can occupy an entire year in a Montessori classroom. All the major civilizations can be connected with this study, since Alexandria was a unique crossroads for most of the major cultures in antiquity, and all

---

107 Ibid., p. 85.

108 Shakrukh Husain (1987), *Demons, Gods & Holy Men from Indian Myths and Legends.* New York: Schocken Books. This is a well-illustrated book with stories that make good reading aloud.

the elements of civilization so richly represented in ancient Egypt can be explored.

Montessori herself saw the value of such an integrated study. "The philosophy of modern history lays emphasis on the meeting and mixing of peoples; groups with tendencies to merge into larger groups, nations at last to start organizing the unity of humanity. Mixing has ever been a slow process, and civilization is its product. Teachers should study the origin, geographical position and growth of each group, its movements and relations with other groups, taking the life history of the whole people rather than individuals."[109]

After Egypt, Montessori explores the contributions of the Mesopotamian civilizations. She talks about their astrology, the Hammurabi laws, the invention of writing on clay tablets, the production of libraries of documents, the walled cities, the flourishing trade, and the Biblical allusions to Babylon.

Montessori then moves on to a discussion of the Persian empire and the reign of Darius, who eventually was challenged by the Greeks. She speaks about the power of Homer's *Iliad* and *Odyssey* and reviews the story of the wars that led to ultimate Greek victory over the Persians—"The mouse had conquered the elephant! . . . Civilization had passed from Asia to Europe."[110]

The children are surprised to learn about pyramids outside Egypt in this study of Mesopotamia. They usually enjoy duplicating the cuneiform writing on clay tablets as a mini-project. Once again, we were fortunate in our school to have a family with Iranian roots. Our study of ancient Persia was made much more concrete and relevant when this family shared some of their culture, customs, and artifacts that had roots in ancient traditions.

Next, Montessori pays tribute to the contribution the ancient Greeks made to the creation of European civilization. She talks about the intellectual freedom of Greece and the philosophy of Socrates, Plato, and Aristotle, the plays of Aeschylus and Euripides, and the discoveries of Eratosthenes and Archimedes.[111] She reviews the exploits of Philip of Macedon and Alexander the Great, ending with only a brief reference to the Roman civilization which

---

109 Maria Montessori, *To Educate*. p. 92.

110 Ibid., p. 103–104.

111 Among other things, Eratosthenes figured out that the world was a sphere, and Archimedes discovered how to calculate the volume of irregular objects by water displacement.

was to follow: "Romans claimed an origin akin to that of the Greeks, and it was to be their task to consolidate the world civilization which the Greek spirit had inspired and created."[112]

Some of the projects connected with Greece and Rome that have enhanced this area of study for our students have included making models of the Acropolis and the Coliseum, a year-long study of Latin for some of our older students, and having Greek and Roman days at the school with costumes and special food. The students also enjoyed having simplified versions of the *Iliad* and the *Odyssey* read aloud to them.

Although Montessori does not devote any chapters of her book to a study of the civilizations of the "New World," it seems obvious to us that any study of Great Civilizations should include at least one of the ancient civilizations of the Americas to round out the survey of the continents of the world. We have usually focused on the Mayan civilization in our school.

As with all these civilizations, literature is a useful complement to the study. For the Mayan culture, Dorothy Rhoads's book *The Corn Grows Ripe,* which won a Newbery Honor in 1957,[113] gives a nice feel of ancient traditions that have been preserved into the present. Also, this study produced our most ambitious overnight field trip—a five-day excursion to the Yucatan peninsula to view the Mayan ruins and enjoy the comfort of a hotel and beach in Cancun, Mexico. It was a surprisingly inexpensive trip from our school near Atlanta.

Montessori's views on history are summarized when she draws on her medical background and compares the flow of history to the development of the various systems of the human organism—generated independently through cell specialization, joined by the circulatory system of the blood, and brought into communication through the nervous system. "The brief review we have taken of the history of human civilization has been meant to show the same basic design at work, for humanity too is an organic unity that is yet being born."[114]

---

112 Maria Montessori, *To Educate,* p. 110.

113 Of the tens of thousands of children's books published each year, only one is chosen for a Newbery Award and one or two others for Newbery Honors. Such awards and critical acclaim in reputable publications help guide us to the best of children's literature for our students.

114 Maria Montessori, *To Educate,* p. 113.

Montessori teachers can approach these civilization studies in many different ways. They can take a survey approach such as that employed by Maria Montessori herself, or they can use a single civilization such as that of Alexandria to focus the study. They can offer traditional lecture presentations of the high points, they can allow the students to research and explore for themselves, or they can create opportunities for dramatizations co-produced by students and teachers. They can use a standard series of questions, based around the fundamental human needs, to guide student research, or they can expand on only the most interesting elements of each civilization studied.

Whatever approach is taken, the important thing to remember is that we are showing children patterns of human life throughout the ages, elements which are common to humans whenever or wherever they live. This insight brings them to a deeper understanding of the contributions of the past to the present, and it leads them to an appreciation of the basic unity of humankind. It is an attempt to further explore the question of "who we are" as humans, today as in the past. It is Cosmic Education!

ONE NATION

In this context, it is possible to study the history of a specific nation without children falling into a nationalistic understanding of the world, as though their nation *is* the world. Each nation can be understood as just one example of the many expressions of human civilization, and each civilization can be understood as just one form of human existence dating back millions of years.

For example, when studying the history of the United States in the proper perspective, it is important not to start with the arrival of the European explorers but to focus attention on the arrival of the first humans in North America. Montessori classrooms can be expected to develop this part of the story in ways that traditional textbook presentations tend to neglect.

The story begins, by most accounts, with the land bridge of Beringia, that Ice Age phenomenon which exposed the sea bottom of the Bering Strait and allowed clans of Asian Cro-Magnons to follow herds of animals onto the American continent. These Paleo "Indians" were big game hunters, and there are fascinating stories to be told about the Clovis, Folsom, and Plano cultures of the Old Stone Age that spread throughout the continent.

Next comes the period of Archaic Indians, those Neolithic communities that developed the Hohokam, Mogollon, and Anasazi cultures in the Southwest, and the Adena, Hopewell, and Mississippian cultures of the mound builders in the East. There is hardly a section of the country that does not have a fascinating collection of archeological sites connected with these ancient cultures.

In our own area, we take a one-day field trip to the Etowah Mounds, near Cartersville, GA, which were constructed centuries before the arrival of the Europeans. When we view artifacts unearthed from some of the mounds, it gives a whole new reality to our studies. We can stand on top of a pyramid of earth erected many hundreds of years ago and imagine what life must have been like for the people of these cultures. As Easterners, we have always been a little envious of schools in the Southwest, who can visit the amazing cliff dwellings of the Anasazi or Pueblo cultures which we can view only in books.

There is a rich story to be told here with the archeological evidence that has been unearthed, a story that is the true foundation of the habitation of North America. The fact that European explorers destroyed most of the culture and many of the indigenous peoples themselves is no excuse for omitting this important chapter in the story of "who we are" in America. We can give our students an awareness of the rich cultures we have squandered and possibly we can restore a remnant of the spiritual symbiosis with nature enjoyed by these peoples. It is time to give a new priority in our classrooms to this early chapter of American history.

Only after this study of ancient Native American civilizations has been thoroughly explored can we begin to talk about the arrival in America of Columbus and other European explorers. Then we can study the colonial period, Revolutionary War, the foundation of the Republic, westward expansion, Civil War, the industrial revolution, the 20th century, and all the other subjects that constitute traditional studies of U.S. history.

These studies can take the form of textbook style presentations or student research, or they can be based on themes—fundamental human needs, territorial expansion, or even foreign relations. The approach is limited only by the amount of creativity and imagination of the Montessori teacher and her students.

One aspect of study that should not be neglected is the rich selection of historical fiction available in the area of American history. We were gratified, for example, to see the heightened interest and understanding of the American Revolution gained by our students from reading aloud the moving story *My Brother Sam is Dead* (winner of a 1975 Newbery Honor).[115] Since there are dozens of books available for almost every period of U.S. history, including some of the most famous and award-winning selections in children's literature, we generally have students read a novel or story of their selection to accompany each chapter of American history.[116]

Whatever the approach and whatever portions of U.S. history are studied, it is all part of exploring in more detail the concentric circle closest to ourselves, the "Who am I?" question at the level of nation. We are all citizens of a particular country, and this too influences what our "cosmic task" might be.

Timelines

The study of civilizations presents a wonderful opportunity for the further development of timelines in a Montessori classroom.

Already in the lower elementary, children are given an idea of how to measure the passage of time, how to count the centuries, and how to distinguish B.C. and A.D.[117] The first application of these ideas into a timeline format beyond a personal timeline is in the study of the Fundamental Needs of Humans, as described earlier.

---

[115] James Lincoln Collier and Christopher Collier (1974), *My Brother Sam is Dead*. New York: Scholastic.

[116] A fuller selection of literature for this study can be found in the *Classroom Resources* appendix in the back of this book.

[117] Some schools use the designation B.C.E. and C.E. for Before the Common Era and the Common Era.

Eventually, as the study moves into specific civilizations of recorded history, time is stated in years with specific names like 1492 A.D. rather than the lengthy and amorphous "periods" and "ages" of our earlier timelines. As students study the ancient civilizations of the world, they can use the Montessori version of the "The Last 10,000 Years of the History of Mankind." Or they can construct parallel timelines, with illustrations of the major contributions of each civilization situated in time to show what was happening simultaneously throughout the world. There are commercial versions of such timelines available in teacher education supply stores to use as models.

Finally, a timeline can be constructed to represent the history of their own nation, with all the stories and interesting facts embedded in the illustrations along the way. This gives them a visual representation of their learning and a tool to pull the entire scope of the story into a whole unit.

As with all previous timelines, the value of this work is to provide a synthesis of learning and a way to put related events and developments in perspective for the students. The more they take an active role in producing these timelines, the more valuable they are.

Conclusion

With this chapter in the story, we have moved finally into the familiar world of "history" as the rest of the educational establishment understands it and as most of us were schooled to see the world and the Universe. Hopefully, our Montessori-educated children will have a totally different perspective on that history, a different appreciation of how far back it can trace its ancestry, and a different experience of what the human race is becoming and what it can potentially be. In other words, history studied in the context of Cosmic Education lets children find further answers for the questions "Who am I? Where do I come from? Why am I here?"

The entire human race has its unique cosmic task. Each individual child we teach has his or her own cosmic task as well.

The Story of the Universe

The Story of the Stars and the Solar System

The Story of the Earth

The Story of Life

The Story of Humans

The Story of Civilization

Montessori and the Future

Peace Education

History

Archaeology

Biology

Geology & Geography

Physics & Chemistry

Metaphysics & Astronomy

Chapter 10

Cosmic Education and the Future

THIS FINAL CHAPTER EXPLORES the implications of Montessori's Cosmic Education for elementary-age children. Why, after all, should we attempt to educate young children this way? What difference will it make in their adult lives and in the future of our planet? What are the positive outcomes of teaching children this way? To answer these questions, we recall Montessori's rationale for Cosmic Education and look at the even more compelling reasons for its relevance today.

Maria Montessori, preoccupied with a world at war, envisioned a future in which education would raise the consciousness of children about the fundamental unity of all human beings, thus making war an absurdity. To attain true peace, she wrote, "we must create a different sort of man in order to have a different sort of society."[118]

Furthermore, she advocated teaching children about the unity that exists at two additional levels—among all living things on Earth and within the Universe itself. The unity of humanity is explored in the Story of Humans, the broad sweep of human history. The unity of all living things is explained

---

118 Maria Montessori, *Education and Peace*, p. xi, translated from the 1949 Italian edition of *Educazione e Pace*.

in the Story of Life, the part of the Montessori curriculum that deals with biogenesis. The unity of the Universe is presented in the Story of the Universe, the ultimate backdrop of cosmogenesis. Cosmic Education is designed to raise children's consciousness of these three basic levels of unity.

This increase in consciousness, according to Montessori, brings about the emergence of a new kind of human being, one who can bring the evolution of our planet to its next stage of development. This is the cosmic task of humanity, to be the conscious witness and promoter of unity for the human race, all of life's forms and the Universe itself. Montessori students are taught to see themselves as citizens of the world, a species within the family of living species on Earth and, ultimately, as descendants of the Universe.

The Unity of Humanity

Montessori first defines our cosmic task as one of creating a utopian harmony within the human race, forging a common consciousness that unites all men and women into one Spirit. In one of her lectures in India in 1946, Montessori stated:

> In the present epoch, the union of all humanity seems to have been reached unconsciously, for today man exchanges not only the produce of his material activity but also the thoughts, the discoveries, and all the products that arise from the work of pure intelligence. One thing is very clear today: that humanity is effectively united. Yet this union was not a conscious task, a conscious aim. . . .
>
> One thing still evades the intelligence of humanity and that is the consciousness of their terrestrial destiny . . . men should, with their conscious will and with their sentiment, seek to find the "adaptation" to present conditions, thus forming one universal harmonious society. . . . But how to attain this if not through a "direct preparation" of the new generation, i.e., through education?[119]

---

119 Maria Montessori, *The Child, Society and the World*, p. 109–110.

It is surprising, almost shocking, to hear Montessori speak of the unity of humanity at a time when World War II was breaking the world apart. Undoubtedly the very fact that it was a "world war" demonstrated her contention that humans were already unified, if only imperfectly and unconsciously.

In her later years, Montessori apparently considered peace education to be her personal cosmic task. Never one to think in small terms, she saw her child-centered education as the way to radically transform society, so that humankind would be protected from the threat of self-destruction through warfare. For this unique approach to peace, she was nominated three times for the Nobel Peace Prize.

Montessori believed that the pursuit of peace begins with the internal development of the child, free from the attempt of adults to dominate and mold the child into their own image. The child's work, in her view, is "the incarnation of human individuality"[120] that takes place as he develops into an adult. This internal development, instead of being natural and unimpeded, is distorted by the warfare adults wage for the soul of the child, seeking to impose on him a depraved morality based on the acquisition of money and unsatisfied pleasure-seeking.[121]

She complained about the "ceaseless war that confronts the child from the very day he is born and is part of his life all during his formative years. This conflict is between the adult and the child, between the strong and the weak, and, we might add, between the blind and the clear-sighted." In this context, she held the child up as "a messiah, as a saviour capable of regenerating the human race and society."[122] Only a new kind of human, based on the natural development of the child freed from adult domination, can root out the fundamental causes of war.

Montessori carried this theme of domination into her discussions of society. In a lecture delivered to the International Office of Education in Geneva in 1932, she challenged the common conception of peace as "the cessation of war." In her view, such a situation represents "the ultimate and permanent triumph of war . . . the forcible submission of the conquered to domination

---

120 Maria Montessori, *Education and Peace*, p. 15.

121 Ibid., p. 13.

122 Ibid., p. 14.

once the invader has consolidated his victory."[123] Her own concept of peace involved a world in which justice and love create harmony among all peoples as they recognize the unity they have already attained.

Montessori described the existing divisions within humanity as meaningless in a future where we travel into the far reaches of space. She asked rhetorically whether any nation can claim the rights to gravity, whether there is any point to a struggle between groups of people in this new cosmic context. She declared that the "two-dimensional history of mankind is now ended,"[124] and we are entering a third dimension as we move off the surface of the Earth and venture into space.

Montessori went on to describe the transformation required for this new stage of society as nothing short of a new stage in evolution. "The crisis we are experiencing is not the sort of upheaval that marks the passage from one historical period to another. It can be compared only to one of those biological or geological epochs in which new, higher, more perfect forms of life appeared, as totally new conditions of existence on earth came about."[125]

Montessori assigned to education the task of bringing about this step forward in evolution. In a 1936 address to the European Congress for Peace meeting in Brussels, Montessori summed up her position: "Preventing conflicts is the work of politics; establishing peace is the work of education."[126]

So why teach Cosmic Education? Montessori would answer that we must teach in this way so the children of today can understand more fully who they are and grow up to create a new kind of society, one in which peace is based on an understanding of the fundamental unity of humanity. In a world in which the threat of nuclear self-destruction was just appearing on the horizon, there was an urgency in her message.

Montessori had a visionary's insight into the future, but the world has changed at an incredible pace since her death in 1952. Rather than invalidating Montessori's teachings about unity, these developments have put us in a position to deepen our consciousness of unity in ways that were not available to Montessori herself.

---

123 Ibid., p. 4–5.

124 Ibid., p. 22.

125 Ibid., p. 23.

126 Ibid., p. 24.

In the political world at the time of Montessori's death, the United Nations was a fledgling organization, the Soviet Union and United States had just launched the Cold War, segregation was the law of the land in the land of the free, and major portions of Africa were still ruled by white men. Economically, the World Bank had just been established, and the growing complexity of international trade did not lead to the establishment of the World Trade Organization until 1995.

In 1952, television was still in its infancy, computers were in the domain of science labs instead of the homes of ordinary people, and telephones were not something you carried around in your pocket. In her own field of medicine, the first diagnosed case of the modern plague of AIDS was still a decade away, it would be 15 years before the first human heart transplant, and there were no machines to take pictures of a functioning human brain.

Yet, the fundamental unity of humanity of which Montessori spoke is all the more evident and impressive in our own day because of these developments and the globalization they have brought about. Ours is a time of global cooperation between governments through organizations like the United Nations; it's a time of global economy, where a jolt on the New York Stock Exchange can be felt around the world; it's a time of global communications, where live coverage is on TV and the touch of a button puts us on the Internet; it's a time of global risk, when excessive consumerism threatens the well-being of the planet and when a virus in one continent can bring the AIDS threat to every nation in the world.

We are one people, one civilization, one humanity, in ways today that Montessori could not even imagine.

THE UNITY OF LIFE

While Montessori spoke and wrote most explicitly and extensively about the unity of the human race, she also alluded to the unity of all life in her writings. In *To Educate the Human Potential*, for example, she speaks about the cosmic task of every living creature and the interdependence of all living things. Her teachings about the unity of all life forms, however, are most clearly defined in the curriculum itself, in the goals implied in the content of the Montessori lessons.

Cosmic Education attempts to establish the oneness of all living things with the Timeline of Life and all the biology presentations found within the Montessori curriculum. The intent of these presentations is to establish the relatedness of all life through a common ancestry, to demonstrate that life in all its forms is simply an extravagant variation on a theme, and to teach young people to respect rather than to exploit other living creatures.

Once again, the discoveries of modern science reinforce these themes. Montessori was a physician with a keen understanding of the workings of the microscopic world of cells and genes, but James Watson and Francis Crick didn't publish their Nobel-prize winning discovery of DNA's molecular structure until the year after her death. We now have a new level of information from DNA and genetic decoding not available to Montessori — a major advance in our ability to demonstrate our fundamental relationship to all other living species. With the analysis of DNA and the molecular comparison of life forms, how could we doubt the unity of all life?

Furthermore, our knowledge of the interdependence of all living things and the delicate balances within the systems of the Earth have grown dramatically during recent decades. In fact, many scientists have begun to speak of Gaia, an understanding of the Earth itself as an organic entity. The Gaia hypothesis "refers to the Earth as having the capacity for *homeostasis*; that is, for comprehensive inner adjustment and self-regulation in response to changes in the outer world."[127]

Such an understanding of genetics and the Earth community creates a new level of consciousness about the unity of all living things that goes beyond what was available to Montessori at the time of her death.

THE UNITY OF THE UNIVERSE

Finally, Montessori education seeks to make students consciously aware of the fundamental unity of the entire Universe. Here, too, Montessori spoke more through the curriculum than any extensive treatise on the subject. The Creation Story and Sun and Earth studies, for example, seek

---

[127] Thomas Berry, *The Great Work: Our Way into the Future*, p. 90.

to give children an understanding of their relationship to everything in the Universe.

When Montessori encouraged us to "give the child a vision of the whole universe," she gave the following rationale: ". . . for all things are part of the universe and are connected with each other to form one whole unity."[128]

Scientific advances since her death bring us into an even deeper consciousness of this Universe connection. Manned space flight has taken us to the moon and to the International Space Station, while the Hubble telescope has allowed us to look millions of light years into the past. This has produced a revolution in our way of thinking about ourselves and the Universe, detailing the story of cosmogenesis and offering us a new level of understanding of our connection to the Universe.

In her book, *Nurturing the Spirit*, Aline Wolf concludes: "If everything in the universe came about from the same source—the original fireball that many believe preceded the creation of the stars—then we as human beings are related to all other human beings, as well as to the animals, plants, oceans and heavenly bodies. Therefore if we deliberately destroy nature or harm other living beings we might be ultimately destroying ourselves. This realization is an underlying principle for promoting peace, equality and care of the earth."[129]

The technological advances, the leaps forward in human knowledge in the years since Montessori's death—all this has changed the world we live in and transformed the answer to the question "Who am I?" We are better equipped today to answer that question, especially in the form of "Where do I come from?" That leaves us to consider the final part of the "Who am I?" question—"Why am I here?"

The Future, Morality, and our Cosmic Task

As we gaze into the future, exciting and alarming at the same time, we are faced with accepting responsibility for shaping that future. Our children have the opportunity of becoming conscious of the fundamental unity of humans, life, and the vast reaches of the Universe. Only with this conscious-

---

128 Maria Montessori, *To Educate*, p. 8–9.

129 Aline D. Wolf, *Nurturing the Spirit*, p. 93.

ness can they create a world that is peaceful for all human beings, as well as respectful of our place in the spectrum of living species and, ultimately, our place in the Universe. Cosmic Education can prepare children to accept this daunting challenge and make the wise choices that will preserve and advance the process of evolution.

Aline Wolf spoke in 2000 at an American Montessori Society conference in New York and talked about the burden we humans bear in the Universe.

> Personally, I find it much more frightening to believe that we are the only example of life in the universe than to believe in aliens living on other planets. While I may be filled with horror at the prospect of a hostile invasion from outer space, I am even more terrified by the awesome responsibility for ensuring the continuation of life on the only planet in the universe where we know it exists.[130]

What if we blow it up, she asks, or let it die by ignoring warnings about the destruction of the ozone layer, global warming, and the poisoning of the oceans? Who will reflect on the wonders of the Universe if we destroy ourselves and our planet?

Love of Humanity—Since Maria Montessori's death, there have been a succession of wars throughout the planet which have pitted against each other political philosophies and economic systems, religions, territorial claims, and even language and cultural backgrounds. Human beings, throughout history, have shown a tendency toward levels of intolerance so strong that war has been the result. In more recent times, this division between human groups has expressed itself in horrible acts of terrorism, such as the September 11, 2001 destruction of the World Trade Towers in New York. We seem to be no closer to true peace than at any time in the past.

Only if we humans can come to respect and celebrate our differences instead of using them as excuses for war and acts of terrorism can we bring peace to our world. Cosmic Education teaches children to recognize the fundamental needs we all share and to respect the cultural differences by which we meet those fundamental needs. Such an education can lead us to a future of true peace such as that sought by Maria Montessori.

---

130 Aline D. Wolf, address to the American Montessori Conference in New York, on March 20, 2000.

Care of Life—Humans, beyond their self-destructive tendencies in war, unquestionably have the power to destroy the fundamental conditions for their own survival on Earth. Most scientists would agree that they have the potential of eradicating life itself on this planet, at least as we know it. The question "Why am I here?" takes on a new urgency in this context, one that was only partially realized during Montessori's time. We have a moral imperative, an important cosmic task, that derives from our deeper understanding of the impact humans are having on the Earth and life.

Thomas Berry, the cultural historian and ecologist, contends that humanity has entered a dangerous phase. As he puts it,

> . . . we have changed the very chemistry of the planet, we have altered the biosystems, we have changed the topography and even the geological structures of the planet, structures and functions that have taken hundreds of millions and even billions of years to bring into existence. Such an order of change in its nature and in its order of magnitude has never before entered either into earth history or into human consciousness.[131]

To deal with these threats to the health of our planet, Berry proposes a system of education based on the story of the Earth and the Universe, similar to the Montessori curriculum of Cosmic Education. "There is need for a program to aid the young to identify themselves in the comprehensive dimensions of space and time (Who am I? Where do I come from?). . . . There is no way of guiding the course of human affairs through the perilous course of the future except by discovering our role (cosmic task) in this larger evolutionary process."[132]

To find our way into the future, it is not sufficient for us to seek guidance from our cultural traditions, he argues. We must go beyond that to our genetic coding, to the planetary community of the Earth, to find our values.

Berry refers to the present as a time of "Great Work" similar to other critical turning points in human history, one that will move the planet from the Cenozoic Era to what he calls the Ecozoic Era. He defines this transition in bold terms: "The Great Work now, as we move into a new millennium, is to carry out the transition from a period of human devastation of the Earth

---

131 Thomas Berry, *The Dream of the Earth*, p. xiii.

132 Ibid., p. 136. Parentheses are our own.

to a period when humans would be present to the planet in a mutually beneficial manner."[133]

Humans need to understand their true place within the community of the Earth. This is morality that goes beyond issues of how humans treat each other and denominational guidelines for human behavior. This is an attempt to build ethical behavior based on our community with all living beings on this planet, and with the Earth itself.

> If the central pathology that has led to the termination of the Cenozoic (era) is the radical discontinuity between the human and the nonhuman, then the renewal of life on the planet must be based on the continuity between the human and the other than human as a single integral community. Once this continuity is recognized and accepted, then we will have fulfilled the basic condition that will enable the human to become present to the Earth in a mutually enhancing manner.[134]

That recognition can only come through an education that emphasizes the unity of all life forces.

Faced with the worldwide problem of toxic poisoning of Earth's air, water, and soil, children who know themselves to be members of the planetary community are more likely to grow up with a mindset to make better decisions for the planet than those raised in a consumerist tradition of conquering and exploiting Earth's resources.

If we think about the daily destruction of thousands of species of living organisms through human expansion, despite the unanswered questions about the effect on our own lives or those of other living creatures, we realize our need for leaders who understand themselves to be members of a single species—albeit a very important one—among many species, each with its own cosmic task on the planet.

In the face of the future potential of genetic research and manipulation, even the potential cloning of humans and production of "designer babies," we want the world to be in the hands of men and women who understand their place in the Epic of Evolution, as described in Chapter 2. We need scientists and entrepreneurs who understand the spiritual side of humanity, educated through Cosmic Education.

---

133 Berry, *The Great Work*, p. 3.

134 Ibid., p. 80.

Respect for the Universe—Berry, like Montessori, goes beyond the confines of our own planet to the Universe as the ultimate context for understanding of ourselves and our cosmic task.

> Our secular, rational, industrial society, with its amazing scientific insight and technological skills, has established the first radically anthropocentric society and has thereby broken the primary law of the universe, the law of the integrity of the universe, the law that every component member of the universe should be integral with every other member of the universe.[135]

Echoing Montessori, Berry urges us to focus education on the Story of the Universe. "Since the universe is an emergent reality the universe would be understood primarily through its story. Education at all levels would be understood as knowing the universe story and the human role in the story."[136] His own connection is primarily with university level education, but Berry acknowledges Montessori's contribution to creating this perspective at the elementary level of education.[137]

What difference will such an education make? We are only in the early stages of understanding our relationship to the Universe. Perhaps humans may be able to affect the Universe itself in ways we do not yet understand. What if we really are the only intelligent life forms in the Universe capable of marveling at its wonders?

If we think about the future of space travel and the possibility of having a direct impact on the Universe or even meeting other life forms, we need to be making that contact with a respect built from an understanding of the unity of the Universe and our place within it. Mike Resnick, an award-winning science fiction writer, follows humans through millennia of future space exploration and conquest in *Birthright: The Book of Man*. Driven by a feeling of superiority and an urge to dominate, humans interact with other intelligent beings throughout our galaxy in successive periods of Republic, Democracy, Oligarchy, and Monarchy until, finally, the rest of the intelligent

---

135 Berry, *Dream of the Earth*, p. 202.

136 Berry, *The Great Work*, p. 81.

137 Ibid., p. 16.

creatures revolt and bring about the destruction of humanity.[138] To avoid such a scenario, we need space travelers and explorers guided by the principles of Cosmic Education.

Conclusion

Montessori developed the concept of Cosmic Education near the end of her own extraordinary life. The world has changed in ways too numerous to fathom since then, but the principles of this educational vision are as valid today as when first formulated. In fact, they have an urgency in the new millennium that did not exist at the time of her death.

Followers of Montessori can take pride in the role Cosmic Education can play in the future of humanity, our planet, and the Universe itself. The curriculum can and should be modernized to reflect the amazing discoveries of modern science, from the macrocosmic world of space to the microcosmic world of genetic engineering. Cosmic Education itself remains as vital today as it was when Montessori first developed it.

---

138 Mike Resnick, *Birthright: The Book of Man*. Although the book is one of futuristic science fiction, we could not help but read it also as an allegory of the domineering and exploitative way the rich and powerful nations of the world like the United States deal with the impoverished countries of the Third World; or, on a more fundamental level, the way humans interact with other species of living things on this planet.

Appendices

1. Scope and Sequence

2. Classroom Resources

3. Glossary

4. References

Scope and Sequence

Montessori's extensive Cosmic Education curriculum is spread over the six years of the elementary level. Careful long-range planning, therefore, is necessary to establish the most practical scope and sequence of the lessons. There is no pre-established progression of lessons. Below is a pattern that we have generally used in our own school. Use it as a guide rather than a dogmatic formula.

In the chart that follows, we have divided the curriculum into six segments representing the six years each child spends in the elementary level. There is a principal story for each year to match Chapters 4–9 in this book. In year 2, the two stories of the Solar System and the Earth are included, and in year 6, we highlighted the Story of One Nation in order to teach American history. Aside from the main focus of each year, we have included other appropriate lessons, particularly from the biology curriculum. The arrows and numbers attached to the lessons show whether they contain elements of a principal story yet to be told in a later year or refer back to one told in a previous year.

In presenting the Great Lessons to our classes—particularly the Creation Story—we have noticed that, although it may be intended primarily for one group of students, other students often join in for the presentation, understanding it in more depth each time they see it.

Regarding years 1–2, some Montessori educators argue that External Parts of Animals and Plants should be presented in the class for three- to

| first semester | second semester |

Year 1 — Story of the Universe

Creation Story
Nature of the Elements
Experiments (study)

Fundamental Human Needs
(vertical studies) → 4-5

External Parts of
Animals and Plants
(label / definition) → 2 ⟶ 3

First Knowledge of
Animals and Plants
(label / Who am I?) → 3

Year 2 — Story of the Solar System | Story of the Earth

Sun and Earth (study)

Composition of the Earth (study)
Work of Air and Water (study)

External Parts of
Invertebrates
(label / definition) → 3

First Knowledge of
Animals and Plants
(question / answer) → 1

External Parts of
Animals and Plants
(cut definition) → 3

Fundamental Human Needs
(horizontal studies) → 4-5

Body Functions of
Animals and Plants
(label / definition) → 3

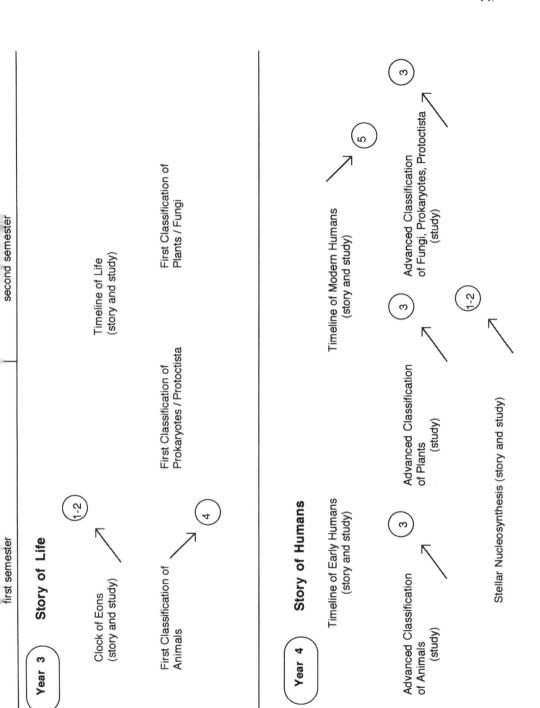

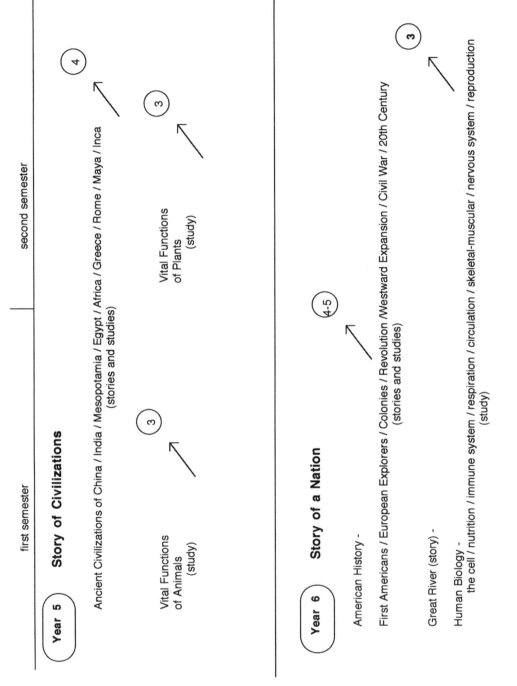

six-year-olds, and there certainly can be an initial presentation of these materials at that level. However, there are several levels of presentation which can enhance the reading program in the lower elementary class and offer numerous chances for children to internalize this fundamental information. Hence, their inclusion here. Multiple levels also exist for First Knowledge, so they can be used for reading in year 1 and research in year 2.

Not all Montessori teachers use External Parts of Invertebrates and Body Functions of Animals and Plants, but both are useful in preparing for later studies in biology and in laying the groundwork for a fuller and deeper understanding of the Story of Life. We think they are most appropriate for students in year 2.

Fundamental Human Needs, which is a first telling of the Story of Humans, can be presented in a vertical study (going back in history with each need) for students in year 1, and in a horizontal study (tracing all the needs in a single civilization) for students in year 2.

It is worth noting that elements of the first five years of study are included in each of the first two years, with references to all of the major stories discussed in Chapters 4–9 and leaving out only American history. Other years also contain references to previous or subsequent years of study. This is one way to teach all of the Great Lessons—and more—without having to present the full stories each time.

The entire year 3 is devoted almost exclusively to the Story of Life, and references to this story are included in every other year of study. The First Classification studies are a perfect complement to the Timeline of Life, with each reinforcing the other. The Clock of Eons provides the link with year 2 studies of the Solar System and the Earth, while First Classification of Animals sets up the Story of Humans in year 4.

In many Montessori classrooms, the Vital Function studies precede the Advanced Classification studies. However, we suggest Advanced Classification studies for year 4 as the perfect complement to studies of Early Humans, in which much time is spent trying to find our closest living and fossil relatives. As for Vital Functions, it is to the animal and plant worlds what civilization studies are to humans.

We suggest a study of American history in year 6 to round out the story at the closest level to our students and to match the curriculum usually found in American elementary schools. Human biology might not seem complementary to American history, but there are some interesting parallels—such as nutrition studies to match the arrival of the First Americans following their food across Beringia; immune system studies to go with the arrival of the Europeans and their deadly diseases; respiration system studies that remind us of the illnesses many colonists suffered and died from in that period; circulation studies that coincide with the bloodshed of the Revolutionary War; skeletal-muscular studies to go with the westward movement of the pioneers; and reproduction studies to match the sexual revolution of the 20th century.

Whenever ties can be made between elements of the curriculum that reinforce each other, the learning is made more effective and interesting. Teachers should always strive to integrate the curriculum elements as much as possible, weaving them into a single fabric.

Classroom Resources

In addition to the references listed within the text of this book, we offer the following selection of classroom resources as a sample of what a Montessori teacher might make available to her students for the various studies. We have gathered them primarily from our own school library and from some other sources,[139] but there are certainly many more valuable resources available. Those listed here are arranged according to the principal story to which they are connected.

I — Story of the Universe

Books

Bailey, Lidia (1982). *The Big Bang: The Creation of the Universe*. Toronto: Annick Press Ltd. Unpaged. Illustrations and simple text provide a picture book to tell the story of cosmogenesis to the youngest students. Lower elementary.

Couper, Heather and Henbest, Nigel (1997). *Big Bang: The Story of the Universe*. New York: Dorling Kindersley. Another story of cosmogenesis in

---

[139] For additional books, we consulted primarily the Wilson Co.'s *Children's Catalog;* for additional videos and CD-ROMs, we consulted libraryvideo.com; for websites, we surfed the Internet.

terms children can understand, with helpful illustrations. Lower and upper elementary.

Dorling Kindersley (1993). *The Eyewitness Visual Dictionary of the Universe.* London: Dorling Kindersley. 64 p. With thousands of terms and illustrations, it's accessible to the youngest elementary students. Lower and upper elementary.

Dorling Kindersley (1999). *DK Space Encyclopedia.* New York: DK Publishing. A comprehensive reference on the world of space, from black holes to stunning Hubble telescope images. Lower and upper elementary.

Fraknoi, Andrew, et al. (1995). *The Universe at Your Fingertips: An Astronomy and Activity Resource Notebook.* San Francisco: Astronomical Society of the Pacific. Project ASTRO notebook, funded by the National Science Foundation and NASA, featuring 90 hands-on activities. Upper elementary.

Henbest, Nigel (1991). *Universe: A Computer Generated Voyage Through Time and Space.* New York: Macmillan. 80 p. Oversized book lets children visit the Big Bang and other events in history of the cosmos. Great timeline in back of book. Lower and upper elementary.

Jedicke, Peter (2003). *Cosmology: Exploring the Universe.* Mankato, MN: Smart Apple Media. 48 p. A discussion of what contemporary science believes regarding the origins and destiny of the Universe, as well as what various peoples have believed throughout history. Lower and upper elementary.

Kerrod, Robin (2003). *Universe* (Eyewitness series). New York: Dorling Kindersley. Explores the Universe from its beginnings, through stars and galaxies, to our own solar system and planets. Lower and upper elementary.

Lippincott, Kristen (2008). *Astronomy* (Eyewitness Science series). New York: Dorling Kindersley. 64 p. Simple text and striking illustrations define basic terms of astronomy, from ancient discoveries to modern advances. Lower and upper elementary.

Morgan, Jennifer (2002). *Born With a Bang—The Universe Tells Our Cosmic Story.* Nevada City, CA: Dawn Publications. 48 p. First part of a trilogy that tells one of the best stories of the Universe for eight- to twelve-year-olds.

Simon, Seymour (1988). *Galaxies.* New York: Morrow Books. Unpaged. An elementary introduction to galaxies in pictures and simple text for the youngest of readers. Lower elementary.

VanCleave, Janice Pratt (1991). *Janice VanCleave's Astronomy for Every Kid: 101 Easy Experiments that Really Work.* New York: John Wiley & Sons. 229 p. Safe, workable astronomy projects that require little in the way of special equipment. Makes learning hands-on, Montessori style. Lower and upper elementary.

Wolf, Aline D. (2000). *I Live in the Universe.* Hollidaysburg, PA: Parent Child Press.

I Look "Out" at the Stars.

I Know What Gravity Does.

How Big is the Milky Way?

I Travel on Planet Earth.

Cosmic Wonder series to introduce children to the Universe and kindle their sense of awe; simple text belies the profound impressions. Lower elementary.

Magazines

Odyssey: Science That's Out of This World. Peterborough, NH: Cobblestone. A real children's magazine for Astronomy. Each of nine annual issues focuses on a different subject. Lower and upper elementary.

Videos

Eames, Charles (1989). *The Films of Charles & Ray Eames: Volume 1 — Powers of Ten.* Santa Monica, CA: Pyramid Media. Striking demonstration of magnitudes, moving outward into deep space by a factor of ten each ten-second frame, then returning to Earth and traveling to the nucleus of a human cell with the same procedure in reverse. Lower and upper elementary.

NASA (1997). NASA Space Series. *Our Universe.* 45 minutes. Examines the Universe with data from space probes and the Hubble telescope, asking tough questions about the mysteries of the Universe. Upper elementary.

Schlessinger Media (1999). Space Science for Children Series. *All About Stars.* 23 minutes. NASA footage and lively animation explores basic questions about the stars. Includes hands-on activities. Lower elementary.

Schlessinger Media (1999). Space Science in Action Series. *Astronomy, Universe, Stars.* 23 minutes each title. Covers topics in more depth for older children than other Schlessinger series. Includes NASA footage and hands-on investigations. Upper elementary.

Silleck, Bayley (1996). *Cosmic Voyage.* IMAX Corp. 40 minutes. Video version of IMAX film nominated for an Academy Award. Uses computer graphics to recreate the birth of the Universe, black holes, and supernovae; "cosmic zoom" effect mimics Powers of Ten. See the IMAX version if you can!

Websites

www.missbarbara.net
  Internet website put together to match the Montessori Great Lessons. Most links go to university sources needing mediation by teacher for younger students. Lower and upper elementary.

www.astrosociety.org/education/
  Site of the Astronomical Society of the Pacific providing educational activities, publications, and resources. Contains special K–12 student section. Lower and upper elementary.

www.amnh.org/explore/ology/astronomy
  Site of the American Museum of Natural History to provide simple information, with cartoon-style drawings, to make astronomy accessible to young children. Lower elementary.

apod.nasa.gov/apod/lib/edlinks.html
  Astronomy Picture of the Day site. Claims to be "topologically complete" in identifying all Internet links for astronomy education. Upper elementary.

www.nasa.gov/audience/foreducators/index.html
   NASA has hundreds of links for the educational community; searches for information regardless of its location within NASA. Lower and upper elementary.

www.zebu.uoregon.edu/disted/ph123/l10.html
   University of Oregon site with a section explaining how the periodic table of elements came about through stellar evolution. Upper elementary.

www.powersof10.com/film
   Website version of the Eames film listed above under *Videos*.

www.micro.magnet.fsu.edu/primer/java/scienceopticsu/powersof10
   Another version of *Powers of Ten* that allows students to manually control the movement from one dimension to the next and study the scale of each level.

www.hubblesite.org/newscenter/archive/releases/2003/27/video/b
   Application of the powers of ten to the emerging Universe from the Big Bang to the formation of our galaxy in an animated version.

www-visualmedia.fnal.gov/VMS_Site/gallery/stillphotos/1999/1100/99-1145D.hr.jpg
   History of the Universe poster showing the early stages after the Big Bang.

www.pa.msu.edu/~baldwin/carol/Lifecycleofstars.swf
   An animation—with dramatic musical accompaniment—to the life cycle of stars.

school.discoveryeducation.com/lessonplans/programs/exploringstars
   Designed for grades 4–6.

www.nasa.gov/connect/artspace/participate/royalty_free_resources.html
   A collection of free images, videos, and very engaging and understandable audio podcasts from NASA to illustrate galaxies, supernova explosions, and lots more.

www.bighistoryproject.com
   This website from the Big History movement is designed for use by high school students but is perfectly appropriate for our upper elementary

students as well. It contains information not only on this chapter but also on all subsequent chapters of the story. Teachers can enhance their own knowledge of the science behind the story and identify specific elements to which students can be directed as they move through the curriculum.

www.chronozoom.com

This website, financed and supported by Microsoft, is an open source, interactive timeline that provides a technologically contemporary way of exploring timelines that fit every stage of the story of Cosmic Education. It is particularly helpful for exploring the early history of the Universe, which is not part of traditional Montessori timelines.

CD-ROMs

Edmark Corp. (2000). *Space Academy GX-1*. WIN95/MAC.
 A great tool for introducing students to the fundamentals of space science. Interactive manipulatives, skill levels, progress tracking, and reference guide. Lower and upper elementary.

Mega Systems (1997). *Cosmos 3D*. WIN 95.
 Designed to answer many of the most common questions about the Universe through 3D animations, graphics, and easy text. Treats origin of the Universe, galaxies, and much more. Lower and upper elementary.

Literature Connections

Hamilton, Virginia and Moser, Barry (1988). *In the Beginning: Creation Stories from Around the World*. San Diego: Harcourt Brace Jovanovich. Illustrated collection of 25 myths from various parts of the world explaining the creation of the world. Suitable for reading aloud to children. Lower and upper elementary.

Hawking, Lucy and Stephen (2007). *George's Secret Key to the Universe*. New York: Simon & Schuster. This first-ever children's book from Stephen Hawking and his daughter, Lucy, is a gripping and funny adventure with lots of fascinating facts about our Universe and the planets. A young boy and his neighbor friend travel through a computer portal into outer space. Lower elementary.

Leeming, David (1994). *A Dictionary of Creation Myths.* New York: Oxford University Press. In dictionary format, compares beliefs about creation in ancient civilizations. Has connections with the Montessori Creation Story and study of civilizations. Upper elementary.

II — Story of the Solar System

Books

Barnes-Svarney, Patricia (1993). *Traveler's Guide to the Solar System.* New York: Sterling Publishing. 80 p. Takes a reader on a tour of the solar system, describing asteroids and each of the planets. Lower and upper elementary.

Branley, Franklyn Mansfield (1988). *The Sun: Our Nearest Star.* New York: Crowell. 31 p. Describes the Sun and how it provides light and energy which allow plant and animal life to exist on Earth. Lower elementary.

Cole, Joanna (1990). *The Magic School Bus Lost in the Solar System.* New York: Scholastic Inc. Unpaged. One of a popular series. Mrs. Frizzle's class goes into outer space and visits each planet in the solar system. Lower elementary.

Daily, Robert (1994). *The Sun.* New York: Franklin Watts. 63 p. Discusses such topics as fusion, the history of astronomy, and parts of the Sun. Clear explanations and striking photographs. Upper elementary.

Gibbons, Gail (1993). *The Planets.* New York: Holiday House. Unpaged. Treats the movements, relative location, and characteristics of the nine planets with simple text and full-color illustrations. Lower elementary.

Gibbons, Gail (1995). *The Reasons for Seasons.* New York: Holiday House. Unpaged. Explains the seasons, the solstices, and the equinoxes through the tilt and orbit of the Earth. Complements Sun and Earth studies. Lower elementary.

Lauber, Patricia (1993). *Journey to the Planets.* New York: Crown. 90 p. Highlights the features of each planet. Uses photographs and information gathered by the Voyager and Magellan explorations. Upper elementary.

Lauber, Patricia (1990). *Seeing Earth from Space.* New York: Orchard. 80 p. Looks at the Earth from the perspective of space through photographs taken by astronauts and satellites. Upper elementary.

Simon, Seymour (1992). *Our Solar System.* New York: Morrow Junior Books. 64 p. With full-color photographs, explores the solar system, including asteroids, meteors, and comets. Simon also did series on each planet. Lower elementary.

Simon, Seymour (1984). *Earth, Our Planet in Space.* New York: Four Winds. Unpaged. Discusses the position of Earth in space and how the days, seasons, and even the topography of the planet are affected. Lower elementary.

Simon, Seymour (2006). *Destination, Space.* New York: Smithsonian/Collins. 30 p. This newly revised exploration of Jupiter, the largest planet in the solar system, provides full-color photos from super telescopes and spacecraft. Readers can journey over the surface of Jupiter, examine its Great Red Spot, and explore the possibility of life on one of its 16 moons. Lower or upper elementary.

Vogt, Gregory (2003). *The Solar System.* Mankato, MN: Capstone Press. 24 p. A simple explanation of the Sun, Moon, and the planets. Learn what the Sun is made of, and how the Sun's gravity makes the planets orbit around it. Find out how far each planet is from the Sun, how many moons it has, and what it looks like up close. Lower elementary.

Wolf, Aline D. (2000). *I Know the Sun Does Not "Set."* Hollidaysburg, PA: Parent Child Press. Cosmic Wonder series. Seeks to reorient the young child's thinking from geocentrism (Earth center) to heliocentrism (Sun center). Lower elementary.

Videos

Dorling Kindersley (1997). *Planets.* 35 minutes.
   Based on the Eyewitness book series, provides a guide to the entire solar system, from Earth to the other planets. Lower and upper elementary.
NASA (1997). NASA Space Series. *Our Solar System.* 45 minutes.
   Explores all the planets of the solar system through Hubble telescope and space probes. Lower and upper elementary.
Schlessinger Media (1999). Space Science for Children Series. *All About the Planets, All About the Sun, All About the Moon.* 23 minutes each. Award-winning video about the planets and critically acclaimed videos about the Sun and Moon for young children. Lower elementary.
Schlessinger Media (1999). Space Science in Action Series. *Sun, Planets & the Solar System, Moon.* 23 minutes each. Another group of highly touted videos that deal with parts of the solar system for older children. Upper elementary.

Websites

In addition to the sites listed with the Story of the Universe, the following websites would be particularly helpful in studies of the Solar System and Planets.

www.nineplanets.org
   A multimedia tour including an overview of the history, mythology, and current scientific knowledge of each of the planets and moons of our solar system. Lower and upper elementary.
www.psi.edu/epo/planets/planets.html
   This is a site of the Planetary Science Institute, out of Tucson, AZ/Laguna Niguel, CA. It deals with all of the planets and the origins of the solar system. Lower and upper elementary.
www.hubblesite.org/newscenter/archive/releases/index/200
   A collection of photos taken by the Hubble Telescope showing details of a variety of scenes from the planets of our solar system to distant galaxies and swirling clouds of matter.

CD-ROMs

Microsoft (1994). *The Magic School Bus Explores the Solar System.* WIN95. A CD-ROM version of Scholastic's popular and instructive series. Provides interactive exploration for the student. Lower elementary.

Literature Connections

Bunting, Eve (1978). *The Island of One.* Mankato, MN: Creative Education. 35 p.

The Mirror Planet
Day of the Earthlings

An asteroid threatens the destruction of the Earth, a televiewer predicts the future, and Earthlings meet Martians in this series. Lower and upper elementary.

III — STORY OF THE EARTH

Books

Branley, Franklyn Mansfield (1990). *Earthquakes.* New York: Crowell. 32 p. Explains what earthquakes are, where they happen, and how they change the Earth. Lower elementary.

Branley, Franklyn Mansfield (1985). *Volcanoes.* New York: Crowell. 32 p. Explains how volcanoes are formed and what happens to the Earth when they erupt. Illustrations are clear and humorous. Lower elementary.

Cole, Joanna (1990). *The Magic School Bus Inside the Earth.* New York: Scholastic. 40 p. Mrs. Frizzle's class learns about different kinds of rocks and the formation of the Earth. Composition of the Earth studies. Lower elementary.

Cole, Joanna (1986). *The Magic School Bus at the Waterworks.* New York: Scholastic. 39 p. Explores the water cycle as Mrs. Frizzle takes her class to clouds, rain, a stream, and pipes leading back to school. Work of Water studies. Lower elementary.

Dixon, Dougal (1991), *The Big Book of the Earth.* New York: Smithmark. 77 p. Divided into sections on the growing planet, the substance of the Earth, the planet's history, changing surface, and our environments. Lower elementary.

Dorling Kindersley (1993). *The Eyewitness Visual Dictionary of the Earth.* New York: Dorling Kindersley. 64 p. Covers such topics as geological time, the rock cycle, minerals, mountain building, erosion, water, atmosphere, and weather. Lower and upper elementary.

Facts on File (2004). *Before Life.* New York: Facts on File. 112 p. Discusses the history of the Earth, exploring the solar system and Earth's position in it, tectonic movements, different types of rocks, and the effects of wind, water, chemicals, and other forces on the surface of the planet. Lower and upper elementary.

Farndon, John (1992). *How the Earth Works: 100 Ways Parents and Kids Can Share the Secrets of the Earth.* Pleasantville, NY: Reader's Digest. Activities related to all aspects of the story of the Earth, including Earth's structure, the violent Earth, rocks, oceans, and atmosphere. Lower and upper elementary.

Gallant, Roy (1986). *Our Restless Earth.* New York: Franklin Watts. 96 p. Geological theories about formation of the Earth and continual changes taking place ever since. Lower and upper elementary.

Javna, John (1990). *50 Simple Things Kids Can Do to Save the Earth.* New York: Andrews and McMeel. Experiments and activities designed to raise consciousness of young children about ecology and to form good habits. Lower and upper elementary.

Maddern, Eric and Duff, Leo (1988). *Earth Story.* Hauppauge, NY: Barron's. 28 p. Tells the story of the Earth from beginnings of the Universe, in beautiful illustrations and simple text. Lower elementary.

Morgan, Jennifer (2003). *From Lava to Life: The Universe Tells Our Earth Story.* Nevada City, CA: Dawn Publications. 48 p. A Montessori classroom-friendly book to tell the story of the development of the Earth and the emergence and evolution of life. Lower elementary.

Simon, Seymour (1991). *Earthquakes.* New York: Morrow Junior Books. Unpaged. Describes how and where earthquakes occur, how they can be predicted, and how they cause damage to human populations. Simon also authored books on *Volcanoes, Mountains,* and *Oceans* with the same publisher. Lower elementary.

Stille, Darlene R. (2007). *Plate Tectonics: Earth's Moving Crust.* Minneapolis, MN: Compass Point Books. 48 p. The tectonic plates that make up Earth's crust are constantly shifting. Throughout history, these plates have collided, moved apart, and slid past one another, resulting in the mountain ranges, islands, and ocean floors. The power of this movement is evident today in violent earthquakes and erupting volcanoes.

Thompson, David (2007). *Processes that Shape the Earth.* New York: Chelsea House. 16 p. Explores Earth's origin, its history over billions of years, and the processes—volcanic eruptions and earthquakes, winds, ocean tides and rivers, shifting continents—that continually shape and sculpt its surface. Lower and upper elementary.

VanCleave, Janice Pratt (1991). *Janice VanCleave's Earth Science for Every Kid: 101 Easy Experiments That Really Work.* New York: John Wiley & Sons. 231 p. Provides young scientists with easy-to-follow instructions for experiments that each introduce a different Earth science concept. Lower and upper elementary.

Van Rose, Susanna (1994). *Earth* (Eyewitness Science series). New York: Dorling Kindersley. 64 p. Deals with formation and composition of Earth, water and oceanography, rocks and minerals, seismology, and formation of mountains. Lower and upper elementary.

Van Rose, Susanna (1992). *Volcano & Earthquake* (Eyewitness book). New York: Alfred Knopf. 61 p. Examines the causes and effects of volcanoes and earthquakes, and it treats historical events as well. Lower and upper elementary.

Videos

Discovery Education (2006). *Earth's Catastrophic Past.* 54 minutes (DVD). Silver Spring, MD: Discovery Communications. Brilliant graphics depict the formation of the oceans, show how volcanoes played a major part in creating the first life forms, bring dinosaurs to life and extinction, and re-create the continental collisions that formed the Himalayas.

NASA (1997). NASA Space Series. *Our Blue Planet.* 45 minutes. Explores what we have learned from weather and communications satellites. Spectral analysis of the environment shows fragility of life. Upper elementary.

Schlessinger Media (1999). Space Science for Children Series. *All About the Earth.* 23 minutes. Covers the whole range of Earth sciences for younger children, with NASA footage, animations, and hands-on activities. Lower elementary.

Schlessinger Media (1999). Space Science in Action. *Earth, Earth's Atmosphere.* 23 minutes each. *Earth* examines what makes our planet so special, composition of the planet, the water cycle, and other topics. *Earth's Atmosphere* looks at function of air. Upper elementary.

Thompson, Francis (1991). *Living Planet.* New York: S. C. Johnson and Son. 39 minutes. Exposes wonders of the natural world and the need to protect and preserve it. Lower and upper elementary.

Websites

education.usgs.gov
  U.S. Geological Service site for education in the fields of geology, biology, geography, and hydrology. Includes section for students with fun projects. Lower and upper elementary.

www.education.noaa.gov
  National Oceanic and Atmospheric Administration resources for education about weather, the environment, and school-based activities. Lower and upper elementary.

serc.carleton.edu/resources/23730.html
   Resources for teaching and learning about Earth system science, and how air, land, water, and life are interconnected. From the Institute for Global Environmental Strategies. Upper elementary.

www.iknowthat.com/com
   A collection of multimedia illustrations to make science and many of the concepts we teach in the Cosmic Education curriculum more understandable and accessible for your students. Treats subjects such as gravity, atoms, vision, volcanoes, earthquakes, human body, sound, cells, solar system, and weather.

www.enchantedlearning.com/subjects/Geologictime.html
   Good site for animation of continental drift and geological time. Also useful for Clock of Eons and Timeline of Life.

school.discoveryeducation.com/lessonplans
   Hundreds of original lesson plans, all written by teachers for teachers. Can browse by subject, grade, or both. K–5, 6–8, 9–12. In addition to Earth Science, subjects include Ancient History, Animals, Astronomy, Geography, Human Body, Physical Science, Plants, U.S. History, and World History.

www.pbslearningmedia.org
   A great site for student browsing of interesting subjects in science for all the chapters of the Cosmic Education story. A handy search feature allows students to zero in on just the information they need, with lots of wonderful NOVA videos and other accessible explanations for complicated concepts. Upper elementary.

CD-ROMs

Microsoft (1997). *The Magic School Bus Explores Inside the Earth.*
   Another of the Magic School Bus series on CD-ROM. Allows interactive exploration and experiments. Lower elementary.

Literature Connections

Caduto, Michael and Bruchac, Joseph (1988). *Keepers of the Earth: Native American Stories and Environmental Activities for Children.* Golden. CO: Fulcrum. Stories to read aloud to sensitize children to the fragility of Earth's natural resources through the eyes of Indian peoples. Lower and upper elementary.

Kraske, Robert (1995). *The Voyager's Stone: The Adventures of a Message-Carrying Bottle Adrift on the Ocean Sea.* New York: Orchard Books. Unpaged. A boy puts a message in a bottle in the Caribbean and a girl living in Australia retrieves it. Explores oceanography and currents. Lower and upper elementary.

IV — STORY OF LIFE

Books

The wealth of books on dinosaurs in prehistoric times and animals of the modern world makes it unnecessary to list separate resources in these areas.

Bender, Lionel (1988). *Plants.* New York: Shooting Star Press. Primitive plants (algae, fungi, mosses, liverworts, ferns), cone-bearing plants, flowering plants. Simple text and illustrations for classification studies. Lower elementary.

Burton, Virginia Lee (1990). *Life Story.* New York: Houghton Mifflin. 72 p. The entire story of biogenesis, written cleverly in the form of a play with eras and periods put into acts and scenes. Illustrated. Lower and upper elementary.

Cole, Joanna (1995). *The Magic School Bus Plants Seeds: A Book About How Living Things Grow.* New York: Scholastic. An easy introduction to the world of plants by Mrs. Frizzle and her class. Lower elementary.

Dixon, Dougal (1990). *The Big Book of the Prehistoric Life.* New York: Gallery. 79 p. Traces the emergence of life from its first beginnings in the seas to the age of man. Tracks Timeline of Life. Lower elementary.

Dorling Kindersley (1995). *The Eyewitness Visual Dictionary of Prehistoric Life.* New York: Dorling Kindersley. 64 p. Divided between plants and animals, with introductory text to set each new time frame. Charts compare population growth and extinctions. Lower and upper elementary.

Gamlin, Linda (1993). *Evolution.* (Eyewitness Science series.) New York: Dorling Kindersley. 64 p. Vividly illustrated guide to the ideas and discoveries that have changed our understanding of the natural world and how life began. Upper elementary.

Hunken, Jorie (1994). *Botany for All Ages: Discovering Nature Through Activities for Children and Adults.* Old Saybrook, CT: Globe Pequot Press. More than 100 botany activities to complement Vital Functions of Plants work and other areas of the Montessori curriculum. Upper elementary.

Jenkins, Steve (2002). *Life on Earth: The Story of Evolution.* New York: Houghton Mifflin. 48 p. Provides an overview of the origin and evolution of life on Earth and of what has been learned from the study of evolution. Lower and upper elementary.

Liebes, Sidney; Sahtouris, Elisabet; and Swimme, Brian (1998). *A Walk Through Time: From Stardust to Us.* New York: John Wiley & Sons. A book about the evolution of life on Earth, arranged with a timeline that elaborates on the Montessori Timeline of Life. Upper elementary.

Lindsay, William (1994). *Prehistoric Life* (Eyewitness Book). New York: Alfred Knopf. 63 p. Uses vivid photos of fossils to explore the record on evolution from very early life forms. Includes ice ages and extinctions. Lower and upper elementary.

McLoughlin, John C. (1981). *The Tree of Animal Life: A Tale of Changing Forms and Fortunes.* New York: Dodd, Mead. 160 p. Discusses the evolution of the major animal phyla through transformations of natural selection acting on genetic material. Lower and upper elementary.

Morgan, Jennifer (2003). *From Lava to Life: The Universe Tells Our Earth Story.* Nevada City, CA: Dawn Publications. 48 p. A Montessori classroom-friendly book to tell the story of the development of the Earth and the emergence and evolution of life. Lower elementary.

Reddy, Francis (1990). *Rand McNally Children's Atlas of Earth through Time.* Chicago: Rand McNally. 77 p. Traces the story of the Universe, the Earth, and life from its beginnings to the present in simple text and drawings. Lower and upper elementary.

Selsam, Millicent Ellis (1978). *A First Look at the World of Plants.* New York: Walker & Co. 32 p. An illustrated introduction to plants, including bacteria, algae, bryophytes, fungi, ferns, gymnosperms, and angiosperms. Lower and upper elementary.

Steel, Rodney, editor (1989). *The Encyclopedia of Prehistoric Life.* New York: Gramercy Publishing. 218 p. Reference-style book that can be used to tie Timeline of Life to classification work. Upper elementary.

Videos

Attenborough, David (1986). *Life on Earth.* Burbank, CA: Warner Home Video. Four hours in two videos. Beautifully photographed and intelligently narrated documentary on the entire Timeline of Life. Organized into easily identifiable segments. Lower and upper elementary.

PBS (1994). Eyewitness Natural World Series. *Fish, Amphibian, Reptile, Bird, Insect.* 35 minutes each title. Selections from the 13-part PBS series exploring the marvels of the natural world. Critical acclaim. Lower and upper elementary.

Schlessinger Media (1999). Animal Life for Children Series. *All About Endangered & Extinct Animals, All About Fish, All About Amphibians, All About Reptiles, All About Birds, All About Mammals, All About Bugs.* 23 minutes each title. Selections from the 13-volume series for young children on a colorful parade of animals, with video field trips and hands-on activities. Lower elementary.

Schlessinger Media (1999). Animal Life in Action Series. *Evolution, Endangered & Extinct Animals, Animal Classification, Insects and Other Arthropods, Marine & Other Invertebrates, Fish, Amphibians, Reptiles, Birds, Mammals, Animal Interdependency.* 23 minutes each title. Selections from a 16-volume series, complements Timeline of Life, Advanced Classification, and Vital Function work for older children. Upper elementary.

Websites

There are some general directories of links to Life Science education sites that could serve as a gateway to this area for the teacher. Two of these are:

www.top20biology.com
www.dmoz.org/Science/Biology/Education

Other useful resources for the teacher in this area are some of the natural history museum sites, which usually carry an education section and some virtual field trips as well. You can look for one specifically in your geographic area or use one of these national resources:

www.mnh.si.edu (National Museum of Natural History in Washington)
www.amnh.org (American Museum of Natural History in New York)
www.fieldmuseum.org (Field Museum of Natural History in Chicago)

There are sites which deal particularly with the controversy surrounding the teaching of evolution vs. creationism:

www.ncse.com
www.talkorigins.org

In addition to the above, the following are some of the most attractive sites we were able to locate for student use in the area of the Story of Life:

www.ucmp.berkeley.edu/exhibits/historyoflife.php
University of California Museum of Paleontology's section called Discovering the History of Life. Links to exhibits on Geologic Time (for Timeline of Life) and Phylogeny (for classification studies). Lower and upper elementary.

geology.er.usgs.gov/paleo/eduinfo.shtml
   Site of the U.S. Geological Survey, contains education resources for paleontology, information on fossils, and a learning web for K–12 education. Lower and upper elementary.

www.amnh.org/explore/ology/paleontology
   Site of the American Museum of Natural History to provide simple information, with cartoon-style drawings, to make paleontology accessible to very young children. Lower elementary.

www.cellsalive.com
   A wonderful, interactive site with animations and webcams showing various aspects of the life of cells. Cell models, mitosis and meiosis, cell cycles, etc.

www.enature.com
   This is a fabulous interactive, online collection of field guides to more than 5,000 species of plants and animals as they are found in nature, acquired by the National Wildlife Federation in 2001. Wonderful for First Knowledge or First Classification work. Students can even narrow the list to animal and plant species found in their zip code and listen to the sounds made by the animals.

www.fi.edu/tfi/units/life/classify/classify.html
   The Franklin Institute presents this awesome site on the classification of plants and animals and other organisms, including Biological Classifications, the Tree of Life, Animal Kingdom Taxonomy, the Diversity of Life, Animal Bytes, and Vascular Vegetables. Enough detail for use at the 9–12 level for Advanced Classification.

www.ucmp.berkeley.edu/exhibits/index.php
   University of California Museum of Paleontology website. Includes sections on the History of Life through Time, a Tour of Geologic Time, Understanding Evolution, the Paleontology Portal, the World's Biomes, and a special K–12 section. Lots of animations, charts, graphs and timelines, etc.

CD-ROMs

Dorling Kindersley (1998) *Amazing Animals.* New York: Dorling Kindersley. Habitats and behavior of interesting array of animals narrated by Henry the Lizard. Good for First Knowledge work. Lower elementary.

Dorling Kindersley (1995). *Eyewitness Encyclopedia of Nature.* New York: Dorling Kindersley. Introduces over 250 plants and animals through video sequences and soundclips. First Knowledge and Classification work. Lower and upper elementary.

Grolier (1994). *Grolier Prehistoria: A Multimedia Who's Who of Prehistoric Life.* Chicago: Grolier. Time tracker, classification, gallery, search, museum, creature show. For Timeline of Life and Classification studies. Lower and upper elementary.

Literature Connections

Caduto, Michael and Bruchac, Joseph (1994). *Keepers of Life: Discovering Plants through Native American Stories and Earth Activities for Children.* Golden, CO: Fulcrum Publishing.

Caduto, Michael and Bruchac, Joseph (1991). *Keepers of the Animals: Native American Stories and Wildlife Activities for Children.* Golden, CO: Fulcrum Publishing. Stories suitable for reading aloud to students to heighten their respect for plant and animal life, with activities suggested for each story. Lower and upper elementary.

Cherry, Lynne (1990). *The Great Kapok Tree: A Tale of the Amazon Rain Forest.* New York: Scholastic Inc. Wonderfully illustrated, easy-read book tells how much life is dependent on trees in the rain forest. Lower elementary.

Dominguez, Angel, illustrator (1991). *Classic Animal Stories.* New York: Arcade. A collection of classic folk tales about animals from Grimm, Chaucer, La Fontaine, Kipling, Aesop, and Joel Chandler Harris. Lower and upper elementary.

Larson, Gary (1998). *There's a Hair in My Dirt.* New York: Harper. Popular cartoonist tells the story of a family of worms, the discovery of a cosmic task and the sometimes strange interactions of humans and other species. Lower and upper elementary.

V — Story of Humans

Books

Allison, Linda (1976). *Blood and Guts: A Working Guide to Your Own Insides.* Boston: Little, Brown and Company. A humorously written book about human anatomy, with lots of experiments to go along with the information. Upper elementary.

Caird, Ron (1994). *Ape Man: The Story of Human Evolution.* New York: Macmillan. 192 p. Examines human evolution by theme such as evolving, walking, thinking, talking, colonizing, making images, and still evolving. Upper elementary.

Coville, Bruce and McDermott, Michael (1990). *Prehistoric People.* New York: Doubleday. 45 p. Traces development from *Australopithecus* to Cro-Magnon, focusing on hunting and farming, artistic endeavors, religious rituals, and technology. Upper elementary.

Grace, Eric. S. (1995). *Apes.* San Francisco: Sierra Club Books for Children. 64 p. Explores the evolution of primates closest to humans, examining similarities and differences between us and them. Lower and upper elementary.

Hurdman, Charlotte (1998). *Step Into . . . The Stone Age.* New York: Lorenz. 64 p. Shows way of life of prehistoric peoples, including migration, social structure, communication, shelter, fire, food, hunting, and first crops. Lower and upper elementary.

Lewin, Roger (1988). *In the Age of Mankind: A Smithsonian Book of Human Evolution.* Washington. DC: Smithsonian Books. 255 p. Includes age of mankind through ancestors and early humans. Lots of photo illustrations. Upper elementary.

Macdonald, Fiona (1998). *The Stone Age News.* Cambridge, MA: Candlewick Press. 32 p. Cleverly presented in the form of a news magazine, covers the appearance of humans as well as their lifestyle. Lower and upper elementary.

Merriman, Nick (1989). *Early Humans* (Eyewitness Series). New York: Alfred A. Knopf, Inc. 63 p. A description of early human origins, tools and weapons, hunting and foraging for food, and the role of family life, money, religion, and magic. Lower and upper elementary.

Morgan, Jennifer (2006). *Mammals Who Morph: The Universe Tells Our Evolution Story.* Nevada City, CA: Dawn Publications. 48 p. A Montessori classroom-friendly book to tell the story of the emergence of humans. This makes a wonderful single-sitting story on the Timeline of Humans. Lower and upper elementary.

Patterson, Francine (1985). *Koko's Kitten.* New York: Scholastic. Unpaged. Real-life story of a gorilla named Koko who learned to use sign language, loved a young kitten, and grieved when the kitten died. Lower and upper elementary.

Sattler, Helen Roney (1988). *Hominids: A Look Back at our Ancestors.* New York: Lothrop, Lee & Shepard. 125 p. The ancestry of humans through the fossil record, with attention to changes in brain size, tooth size and function, bipedalism, and toolmaking. Upper elementary.

Tattersall, Ian (1993). *The Human Odyssey: Four Million Years of Human Evolution.* New York: Prentice Hall. 191 p. The curator of the American Museum of Natural History tells the story in a way that matches the Montessori curriculum, although in much greater detail. Upper elementary.

Videos

A&E (1994). *Ape Man: The Story of Human Evolution.* 50 minutes. A four-volume exploration of the evolution of humans, narrated by Walter Cronkite. Upper elementary.

Johanson, Don. *In Search of Human Origins. Episode one: The Story of Lucy.* NOVA production/by Green Umbrella Ltd. and WGBH Science Unit, in association with the Institute of Human Origins and BBC-TV. Johanson recounts how he unearthed Lucy in 1974, an almost 3-million-years-old human ancestor who walked upright. Upper elementary.

Websites

www.humanorigins.si.edu
   The Smithsonian's Museum of Natural History explores early humans and their ancestors with photos, family trees, and a section for posing questions. Upper elementary.

www.pbs.org/wgbh/aso/tryit/evolution
   Explores when humans evolved, who their ancestors were, and why these species adapted. Includes Shockwave game. Upper elementary.

www.becominghuman.org
   Becoming Human is an interactive documentary experience that tells the story of our origins. Journey through four million years of human evolution with your guide, Donald Johanson. Upper elementary.

www.anth.ucsb.edu/projects/human
   This University of California, Santa Barbara site is an online 3D gallery of modern primate relatives and fossil ancestors of humans. The gallery contains five modern primate crania and five fossil crania. The crania can be rotated 360 degrees. Each cranium is accompanied by a short description of its relevance to human evolution and a site map.

Literature Connections

Cowley, Marjorie (1994). *Dar and the Spear Thrower.* New York: Houghton Mifflin. 118 p. A young Cro-Magnon boy is initiated into manhood by his clan and sets off to trade his fire rocks for an ivory spear thrower. Upper elementary.

Crompton, Anne Eliot (1971). *The Sorcerer.* Boston: Little, Brown. 175 p. Useless to his tribe after being injured by a bear, a prehistoric youth discovers he has the power to capture on cave walls the shape and spirit of the various animals he sees. Upper elementary.

Denzel, Justin (1988). *Boy of the Painted Cave.* New York: Putnam. 158 p. Forbidden to make images, a 14-year-old boy with a bad foot yearns to be a cave painter. Upper elementary.

Hoff, Syd (1992). *Stanley.* New York: Harper Collins. 64 p. Chased away by the other cavemen because he is different, Stanley finds a new and better way of living.

Shykoff, Henry (1999). *Once Upon a Time, Long, Long Ago.* Toronto: Natural Heritage/Natural History. 111 p. The story of a sister and brother that fits in what we know about what it meant to be human 50,000 years ago. Upper elementary.

Steele, William (1979). *The Magic Amulet.* New York: Harcourt Brace Jovanovich. 114 p. Left to die by his prehistoric family band, a wounded young hunter must find and join a new group if he is to survive. Story takes place in prehistoric America. Upper elementary.

Treece, Henry (1967). *The Dream Time.* New York: Meredith Press. 114 p. Crookleg, a Stone Age boy, finds that the people of his clan fear his talent for drawing and shaping figures from clay. After his family is killed in a fight with another clan, he wanders from tribe to tribe in search of understanding. Upper elementary.

Turnbull, Ann (1984). *Maroo of the Winter Caves.* New York: Houghton Mifflin. 136 p. A young girl in the late Ice Age must take charge when her father is killed and lead her family to winter camp before the blizzards strike. Upper elementary.

Turner, Ann Warren (1987). *Time of the Bison.* New York: McMillan. 54 p. Eleven-year-old Scar Boy, one of a group of primitive cave dwellers, discovers that he has a gift for making pictures and becomes an apprentice to Painter of Caves. Lower and upper elementary.

VI — STORY OF CIVILIZATIONS

Books

Adams, Brian et al. (1994). *Encyclopedia of Great Civilizations.* New York: Shooting Star Press. Illustrated studies of Egypt, China, Japan, Greece, Rome, the Vikings, the Aztecs, and the Incas. Lower and upper elementary.

Briquebec, John (1990). *The Ancient World: From the Earliest Civilizations to the Roman Empire.* New York: Warwick Press. 320 p. Describes historical and social events from era of prehistoric people through the fall of the Roman Empire. Upper elementary.

Cotterell, Arthur (1994). *Ancient China* (Eyewitness series). New York: Alfred A. Knopf, Inc. 63 p. A photo essay documenting ancient China from Confucius to paper, medicine, dress, and festivals. Lower and upper elementary.

Delf, Brian (1995). *In the Beginning . . . The Nearly Complete History of Almost Everything.* New York: Dorling Kindersley. 76 p. Sections on everyday life — homes, clothing, medicine, weapons — buildings and transportation. Great for Fundamental Human Needs. Lower elementary.

Dorling Kindersley (1994). *The Eyewitness Visual Dictionary of Ancient Civilizations.* New York: Dorling Kindersley. 64 p. Illustrations and simple text on civilizations including Mesopotamia, Egypt, Assyria, Babylon, Persia, Greece, Rome, India, and China. Lower and upper elementary.

Ganeri, Anita (1994). *Focus on Ancient Egyptians.* New York: Shooting Star Press. 32 p. Uses simple text and illustrations to describe this ancient civilization. Other volumes available on Vikings, Romans, Greeks, Aztecs, and Incas. Lower and upper elementary.

James, Simon (1990). *Ancient Rome* (Eyewitness series). New York: Alfred A. Knopf, Inc. 48 p. A photo essay documenting ancient Rome and the people who lived there as revealed through the many artifacts they left behind. Lower and upper elementary.

Kingfisher (2002). *Everyday Life in the Ancient World*. Boston: Kingfisher. 128 p. Describes the everyday life of ancient Egyptians, Greeks, Romans, Aztecs, and Incas, including transportation, clothing, food, homes, shopping, and monuments.

Martell, Hazel Mary (1995). *The Kingfisher Book of the Ancient World.* New York: Kingfisher. 159 p. From the Ice Age to the Fall of Rome. Big print, simple text, illustrations focus on government and rulers of traditional history. Lower and upper elementary.

Millard, Anne (1994). *The Atlas of Ancient Worlds.* New York: DK Publishing. A geographic complement to civilization studies. Lower and upper elementary.

Millard, Anne (1985). *The Usborne Book of World History.* London: Usborne. 195 p. An introduction to world history from the first civilizations to the 20th century. another good resource for Fundamental Human Needs. Lower elementary.

Pearson, Anne, and Nicholls, Nick (1992). *Ancient Greece.* (Eyewitness series.) New York: Alfred A. Knopf Inc. 63 p. Photo essay documenting ancient Greece, including the land, history, and elements of civilization. Lower and upper elementary.

Odijk, Pamela (1989). *The Egyptians.* Englewood Cliffs, NJ: Silver Burdett. 47 p.
(1989) *The Romans.*
(1989) *The Greeks.*
(1989) *The Phoenicians.*
(1990) *The Vikings.*
(1990) *The Israelites.*
(1990) *The Mayas.*
(1990) *The Incas.*
(1991) *The Chinese.*
(1991) *The Japanese.*

Series deals with the daily life of ordinary people in addition to the big figures of history, much the way Montessori approached history. Upper elementary.

Scarre, Chris (1993). *Smithsonian Timelines of the Ancient World: A Visual Chronology from the Origins of Life to AD 1500.* New York: DK Publishing. A useful tool for construction of timelines in civilization studies. Includes side-by-side historical developments by continent in timeline form. Upper elementary.

Somerset Fry, Plantagenet (1994). *History of the World.* New York: Dorling Kindersley. 383 p. Bite-size lessons in world history from prehistoric times through 20th century. Illustrations and simple text, with comparative timelines. Upper elementary.

Magazines

Calliope: World History for Young People. Peterborough, NH: Cobblestone. A children's magazine for World History. Each of the five annual issues focuses on a different subject. Upper elementary.

Videos

Schlessinger Media (1998), Ancient Civilizations for Children Series. *Ancient China, Ancient Mesopotamia, Ancient Egypt, Ancient Greece, Ancient Rome, Ancient Aegean, Ancient Africa, Ancient Maya, Ancient Inca.* 23 minutes each title. Like Montessori, this made-for-student series focuses on ordinary people and ways of life as much as the big events and leaders. Upper elementary.

Websites

www.cybersleuth-kids.com/sleuth/History/Ancient_Civilizations
  A comprehensive educational directory, research tool, and homework helper that provides a wide variety of resources on ancient civilizations from every continent and part of the world. Upper elementary.

www.crystalinks.com/ancient.html
  Provides information on and discussion of dozens of ancient civilizations from throughout the world, with a wealth of pictures, maps, and illustrations to make it all accessible for young researchers. Upper elementary.

www.pbs.org/empires/egypt/index.html
  Everything you ever wanted to know about Ancient Egypt, in an interactive format that allows student exploration. Lower and upper elementary.

www.pbs.org/empires/egypt/special/lifeas
  Information on a day in the life of various people in ancient Egypt—a pharaoh, a nobleman, a craftsman, a priest, a soldier, a farmer, and a woman. Other sections on this "special" site (leave off "lifeas") deal with hieroglyphics, a timeline, and a virtual Egypt tour which allows interactive, 360-degree views of the remains of ancient sites. Lower and upper elementary.

CD-ROMs

Cambridge (1999). *Ancient History CD-ROM Series.*
  Engaging characters, virtual environments and simulations that lead into Egypt, Greece, and Rome. Upper elementary.

Entrex (1997). *Ancient Civilizations.*
  Simulation activities within the context of a variety of ancient civilizations makes this a tool for exploring daily life, major events, and important people. Lower and upper elementary.

Sumeria (1999). *Exploring Ancient Cities.*
  Tours the excavated ruins of Pompeii, Crete, Petra, and Teotihuacan as a vehicle for exploring ancient civilizations. Upper elementary.

Literature Connections

Chandon, G. (1964). *Stories from the Aeneid*. New York: World Publishing. 190 p. A young reader's version of the famous stories from the *Aeneid* in Roman literature. Upper elementary.

Divin, Marguerite (1978). *Stories From Ancient Egypt*. New York: Burke Publishing. A selection of stories for reading aloud or exploring alone. Upper elementary.

Gregory, Kristiana (1999). *Cleopatra VII, Daughter of the Nile, Egypt, 57 B.C.* (Royal Diaries series). New York: Scholastic. 221 p. With her father in hiding after assassination attempts, 12-year-old Cleopatra records in her diary her fears for her own safety and hopes to be queen. Upper elementary.

Husain, Shahrukh (1987). *Demons, Gods & Holy Men from Indian Myths and Legends.* New York: Schocken Books. 132 p. Myths and traditional tales from the ancient civilization of the Hindus and other peoples of India. Suitable for reading aloud. Upper elementary.

Lasky, Katheryn (1994). *The Librarian who Measured the Earth.* Boston: Joy Street Books. 48 p. Describes the life and work of Eratosthenes, the Greek geographer and astronomer who accurately measured the circumference of the Earth. Lower and upper elementary.

McKissack, Pat (2000). *Nzingha, Warrier Queen of Matamba Angola, Africa, 1595* (Royal Diaries series). New York: Scholastic. 136 p. The diary of a 13 year-old West African princess who loves to hunt and hopes to lead her kingdom one day against slave traders. Upper elementary.

Richardson, I. M. and Frenck, Hal (1984). *Odysseus and the Giants.* Mahwah, NJ: Troll. 31 p. From Greek literature, Odysseus relates to his listeners his fleet's experiences on the Island of the Winds and with the man-eating Giants. Upper elementary.

Rhoads, Dorothy (1956). *The Corn Grows Ripe.* New York: Viking Press. 88 p. Newbery Honor 1957. The story of a young Mayan boy who must take his injured father's place in raising the annual crop of corn. Upper elementary.

Snyder, Zilpha Keatley (1967). *The Egypt Game.* New York: Yearling. Newbery 1968. The story of two girls who find out they both love anything to do with ancient Egypt and start a club to play the Egypt game. Upper elementary.

Speare, Elizabeth George (1961). *The Bronze Bow.* Boston: Houghton Mifflin. 255 p. When the Romans brutally kill Daniel bar Jamin's father, the young Palestinian searches for a leader to drive them out, but comes to realize that love may be a more powerful weapon than hate. Newbery Medal winner. Upper elementary.

VII — STORY OF ONE NATION

Books

Altman, Susan (1989). *Extraordinary Black Americans from Colonial to Contemporary Times.* Chicago: Children's Press. 240 p. Short biographies of black Americans who contributed to the growth of American society by their personal achievements. Upper elementary.

Archer, Jules (1991). *Breaking Barriers—The Feminist Revolution.* New York: Puffin. 207 p. An exploration of the women's movement and the women who created it, from Susan B. Anthony to Betty Friedan. Upper elementary.

Brenner, Barbara (1994). *If You Were There in 1776.* New York: Simon & Schuster. 135 p. Shows how concepts in the Declaration of Independence grew out of experiences of living in America, with emphasis on children. Upper elementary.

Freedman, Russell (1983). *Children of the Wild West.* New York: Scholastic. 95 p. What did children of pioneer families experience as they traveled west in a wagon train? A photo essay. Upper elementary.

Freedman, Russell (1985). *Cowboys of the Wild West.* New York: Clarion Books. 101 p. Explores what life was like for the real-life cowboys of the old West. Upper elementary.

Freedman, Russell (1987). *Indian Chiefs.* New York: Holiday House. 150 p. Biographies of six Indian chiefs who led their people at historic moments as pioneers encroached on their hunting grounds. Upper elementary.

Gross, Belov Ruth (1982). . . . *If You Grew Up With George Washington.* New York: Scholastic. 80 p. Tells what it was like to live in Virginia during the colonial times of the 1730s and 1740s. Lower and upper elementary.

Howarth, Sarah (1994). *Colonial People.* New York: Simon & Schuster. 47 p. Describes the everyday lives of thirteen colonial people through the use of quotations and illustrations of the time. Upper elementary.

Lester, Julius (1968). *To Be a Slave.* New York: Scholastic. 156 p. Newbery Honor 1969. The non-fiction story of slavery, told through the men and women who lived through it. Upper elementary.

Levine, Ellen (1992). . . . *If You Traveled West in a Covered Wagon.* New York: Scholastic. 80 p. Tells what it was like to be a pioneer and travel West to Oregon in the 1840s. Lower and upper elementary.

Maestro, Betsy and Giulio (1990). *The Discovery of the Americas.* New York: Lothrop. 48 p. Discusses both hypothetical and historical voyages to America by the Phoenicians, Vikings, and later European explorers. Upper elementary.

McGovern, Ann (1964). . . . *If You Lived in Colonial Times.* New York: Scholastic. 80 p. Tells what it was like to live in the New England colonies during the years 1565 to 1776. Lower and upper elementary.

McGovern, Ann (1966). . . . *If You Grew Up with Abraham Lincoln.* New York: Scholastic. 80 p. What it was like to grow up on the frontiers of Kentucky, Indiana, and Illinois. Lower and upper elementary.

Payne, Elizabeth Ann (1966). *Meet the Pilgrim Fathers.* New York: Random House. 86 p. Tells about why the Separatists left England, their journey on the Mayflower, first winters in New England, and Thanksgiving. Lower and upper elementary.

Richards, Kenneth (1970). *The Story of the Conestoga Wagon.* Chicago: Children's Press. 30 p. Traces the history of the wooden wagons that served as the major means of transportation for going west for 100 years. Lower and upper elementary.

Sattler, Helen Roney (1993). *The First Americans.* New York: Houghton Mifflin. 125 p. Covers the history of early humans in America from the earliest known sites to the time of the arrival of the first European settlers. Upper elementary.

Sansevere-Dreher, Diane (1992). *Explorers Who Got Lost.* New York: Tom Doherty Associates. 135 p. Tells the stories of explorers who lucked into discoveries, from Diaz to Da Gama, Columbus, Cabot, Magellan, Verrazano, Cartier, and Hudson. Upper elementary.

Sinnott, Susan (1991). *Extraordinary Hispanic Americans.* Chicago: Children's Press. 277 p. Profiles the lives of Hispanics who helped shape the history of the United States, from the early explorers to the 20th century. Upper elementary.

Wingate, Philippa (1998). *Who Were the First Americans?* Tulsa, OK: Educational Development Corp. 32 p. An illustrated book showing different groups of Native Americans and how they lived. Text is simple and descriptive of the pictures. Lower and upper elementary.

Magazines

Cobblestone: the History Magazine for Young People. Peterborough, NH: Cobblestone. A children's magazine for American history. Each of the nine annual issues focuses on a different subject. Upper elementary.

Videos

Schlessinger Media (1996). United States History Video Collection. *Three Worlds Meet: Origins—1620.* 35 minutes. First in a 20-volume series of videos for grades 5–12 in the study of American History. Thoroughly researched and attractive format. Other titles go through all of U.S. history, up to year 2000 with recent additions. Upper elementary.

Burns, Ken (1990). *The Civil War.* New York: PBS Home Video.
Nine-volume video series, geared to adult audiences and far too detailed for general classroom use. Introductory episode useful in talking about the causes of the war, and rest can be made available to interested students. Upper elementary.

CD-ROMs

A.D.A.M. Software. *A.D.A.M. The Inside Story.* Atlanta: ADAM Software. "Animated Dissection of Anatomy for Medicine" creates the acronym for the main character who tells the story of the human body in clever dialogue without sacrificing accuracy. Popular resource for human biology. Upper elementary.

Creative Multimedia. *Smithsonian's America: An Interactive Exploration of American History and Culture.* Washington, D.C. A virtual museum of American history artifacts and sounds from the past, including some important speeches and other actualities. Upper elementary.

Websites

www.socialstudiesforkids.com/subjects/ushistory.htm
A comprehensive site, designed for use by students, covering the whole scope of American history, from the first Americans to modern times. Includes teacher resources and timelines. Upper elementary.

www.ushistory.org
The Independence Hall Association owns this website, which supports its mission to educate the public about the Revolutionary and Colonial eras of American history, as well as Philadelphia generally. Also covers other periods of U.S. history in an easily searchable online textbook, and provides links to other sites. Upper elementary.

www.mrnussbaum.com/history
  An interactive site that allows students to explore specific topics in American history, with elementary-friendly content and embedded short videos.

Literature Connections

Because of the rich selection of historical fiction in this area and the opportunity to excite 6th-grade students with good literature, we offer an expanded—but by no means exhaustive—selection of books in this section, organized by time period or theme.

European Exploration

Conrad, Pam (1991). *Pedro's Journal: A Voyage with Christopher Columbus.* New York: Apple. 80 p.

Colonial Period

Clapp, Patricia (1982). *Constance, A Story of Early Plymouth.* New York: Beech Tree Books. 255 p.

Fleischman, Paul (1990). *Saturnalia.* New York: Harper. 112 p.

Lasky, Kathryn (1995). *A Journey to the New World: The Diary of Remember Patience Whipple—Mayflower, 1620.* New York: Scholastic. 172 p.

Rinaldi, Ann (2000). *The Journal of Jasper Jonathan Pierce, a Pilgrim Boy—Plymouth, 1620.* New York: Scholastic. 154 p.

Speare, Elizabeth George (1984). *The Sign of the Beaver.* New York: Dell. Newbery Honor.

Revolutionary War

Collier, James Lincoln (1983). *War Comes to Willy Freeman.* New York: Dell. 178 p.

Collier, James Lincoln and Christopher (1975). *My Brother Sam is Dead*. New York: Scholastic. Newbery Honor.

Denenberg, Barry (1998). *The Journal of William Thomas Emerson, a Revolutionary War Patriot — Boston, Massachusetts, 1774*. New York: Scholastic. 156 p.

Forbes, Esther (1943). *Johnny Tremain: A Novel for Old and Young*. Boston: Houghton Mifflin Co. 256 p. Newbery Award.

Fritz, Jean (1987). *Early Thunder*. New York: Puffin Books. 255 p.

Gregory, Kristiana (1996). *The Winter of Red Snow: The Revolutionary War Diary of Abigail Jane Stewart — Valley Forge, Pennsylvania*. New York: Scholastic. 170 p.

Griffin, Judith Berry (1977). *Phoebe the Spy*. New York: Scholastic. 47 p.

Haynes, Betsy (1974). *Spies on the Devil's Belt*. New York: Apple. 158 p.

O'Dell, Scott (1980). *Sarah Bishop*. New York: Scholastic. 250 p.

Rinaldi, Ann (1986). *Time Enough for Drums*. New York: Troll. 246 p. ALA Best Book.

The Pioneers

Brenner, Barbara (1993). *Wagon Wheels*. New York: Harper Collins. 64 p.

Brink, Carol R. (1936). *Caddie Woodlawn*. Newbery Award.

Cather, Willa (1954). *My Antonia*. Boston: Houghton Mifflin Co. 372 p.

Cushman, Karen (1996). *The Ballad of Lucy Whipple*. New York: Clarion Books. 195 p.

DeFelice, Cynthia (1991). *Weasel*. New York: Avon Camelot. 119 p.

Durbin, William (1999). *The Journal of Sean Sullivan, a Transcontinental Railroad Worker — Nebraska and Points West, 1867*. New York: Scholastic. 184 p.

Fleischman, Sid (1992). *Jim Ugly*. New York: Yearling. 130 p.

Gregory, Kristiana (1996). *Across the Wide and Lonesome Prairie: The Oregon Trail Diary of Hattie Campbell, 1847*. New York: Scholastic. 164 p.

Gregory, Kristiana (1999). *The Great Railroad Race: The Diary of Libby West—Utah Territory, 1868.* New York: Scholastic. 201 p.

James, Will (1954). *Smoky the Cow Horse.* New York: Scholastic. 310 p. Newbery Award 1927.

MacLachlan, Patricia (1984). *Sarah, Plain and Tall.* New York: Harper. 58 p. Newbery Award.

Meyer, Carolyn (1992). *Where the Broken Heart Still Beats: The Story of Cynthia Ann Parker.* New York: Harcourt. 194 p.

Wilder, Laura (1953). *Little House on the Prairie.* New York: Scholastic.

Wilder, Laura (1953). *Little Town on the Prairie.* New York: Scholastic. 288 p. Newbery Honor 1942.

Slavery

Berry, James (1991). *Ajeemah and His Son.* New York: Harper. 83 p. Horn Book Award.

Chambers, Veronica (1998). *Amistad Rising: A Story of Freedom.* San Diego: Harcourt Brace & Co. 37 p.

Collier, James Lincoln (1981). *Jump Ship to Freedom.* New York: Dell. 198 p.

Collier, James Lincoln (1984). *Who is Carrie?* New York: Dell. 158 p.

Fox, Paula (1973). *The Slave Dancer.* New York: Dell. 152 p. Newbery Award.

Hamilton, Virginia (1988). *Anthony Burns: The Defeat and Triumph of a Fugitive Slave.* New York: Alfred A. Knopf. 193 p.

Paulsen, Gary (1993). *Nightjohn.* New York: Laurel Leaf. 92 p.

Rinaldi, Ann (1991). *Wolf by the Ears.* New York: Scholastic. 250 p. ALA Best Book.

Sterne, Emma Gelders (1953). *The Slave Ship.* New York: Apple. 188 p.

Yates, Elizabeth (1989). *Amos Fortune—Free Man.* New York: Puffin Books. 181 p. Newbery Award 1951.

Civil War

Alcott, Louisa May et al. (1988). *Civil War Women.* New York: Simon & Schuster. 175 p.

Beatty, Patricia (1987). *Charley Skedaddle.* New York: Troll. 186 p.

Beatty, Patricia (1991). *Turn Homeward, Hannalee.* New York: Troll. 193 p.

Beatty, Patricia (1991). *Be Ever Hopeful, Hannalee.* New York: Troll. 216 p.

Crane, Stephen (1968). *The Red Badge of Courage.* New York: Golden Press. 190 p.

Denenberg, Barry (1996). *When Will This Cruel War be Over? The Civil War Diary of Emma Simpson—Gordonsville, Virginia, 1864.* New York: Scholastic. 156 p.

Hesse, Karen (1999). *A Light in the Storm: The Civil War Diary of Amelia Martin—Frederick Island, Delaware, 1861.* New York: Scholastic. 169 p.

Hunt, Irene (1965). *Across Five Aprils.* New York: Grosset & Dunlap. 190 p. Newbery Honor.

Keith, Harold (1987). *Rifles for Watie.* New York: Harper. 332 p. Newbery Award 1957.

Rinaldi, Ann (1993). *In My Father's House.* New York: Scholastic. 312 p. ALA Best Book.

Immigration

Bartoletti, Susan Campbell (2000). *A Coal Miner's Bride: The Diary of Anetka Kaminska—Lattimer, Pennsylvania, 1896.* New York: Scholastica. 219 p.

Hesse, Karen (1993). *Letters from Rifka.* New York: Puffin Books. 145 p. ALA Notable Book.

Levine, Ellen (1989). *I Hate English.* New York: Scholastic.

Polacco, Patricia (1988). *The Keeping Quilt.* New York: Simon & Schuster.

Yep, Laurence (2000). *The Journal of Wong Ming-Chung, a Chinese Miner—California 1852.* New York: Scholastic. 218 p.

World Wars

Bunting, Eve (1995). *Spying on Miss Muller*. New York: Clarion. 179 p.

Cormier, Robert (1998). *Heroes*. New York: Delacorte. 135 p.

Denenberg, Barry (2000). *One Eye Laughing, the Other Weeping: The Diary of Julie Weiss, Vienna, Austria, to New York, 1938*. New York: Scholastic. 250 p.

Denenberg, Barry (1999). *The Journal of Ben Uchida, Citizen 13559, Mirror Lake Internment Camp—California, 1942*. New York: Scholastic. 154 p.

Greene, Bette (1993). *Summer of My German Soldier*. New York: Bantam. 199 p. ALA Notable Book.

Levitin, Sonja (1970). *Journey to America*. New York: Scholastic.

Lowry, Lois (1990). *Number the Stars*. New York: Dell. 137 p. Newbery Award.

Myers, Walter Dean (1999). *The Journal of Scott Pendleton Collins, A World War II Soldier—Normandy, France, 1944*. New York: Scholastic. 137 p.

Osborne, Mary Pope (2000). *My Secret War: The World War II Diary of Madeline Beck—Long Island, New York, 1941*. New York: Scholastic. 182 p.

Glossary

Adena—A group of Archaic "Indians" who lived in the Ohio Valley and who were among the mound-builders in North America.

Advanced Classification—The part of the Montessori biology curriculum that deals with the taxonomy or classification of the five kingdoms, particularly for the older children of upper elementary.

Amphibians—The first animals with a backbone to emerge from exclusive life in the seas, characterized by part of their life spent in water and part on land.

Anasazi—A group of Archaic "Indians," also known as Pueblo people, who were among the first farmers in North America and who lived in cliffside dwellings in the Southwest.

Anthropomorphism—The ascribing of human characteristics to things that are not human, particularly in the description of the deity.

Archeon Eon—The time of "ancient life," when megamolecules formed that generated bacteria and made later life possible (from 3.8 billion to 2.5 billion years ago). Represented in gray on the Clock of Eons.

Arthropods (Arthropoda)—Animals without a backbone characterized by jointed limbs and including insects as one of the largest groups in classification studies.

Aurignacians—A Paleolithic group of humans who lived in modern-day France and decorated the insides of caves with colorful paintings of the animals they hunted.

Australopithecus—An extinct hominid or human-like creature. The root "pithecus" comes from the Greek word for ape, while "australo" is derived from the Greek word for southern.

Azilians—People of the Mesolithic period who lived in the forests of Europe and invented the bow and arrow, with fine points called microliths.

Beringia—The Ice Age phenomenon that exposed the sea bottom of the Bering Strait and allowed early humans to follow herds of animals from eastern Asia to North America.

Big Bang—The common term for the beginning of the Universe, believed to be an outburst of pure energy into space that gradually changed into matter and led to an expanding Universe.

Biogenesis—The most common understanding of the term "evolution," or the scientific theory for the formation and development of the various life forms on Earth. A word of Greek origin meaning "life-birth."

Biosphere—The realm of living organisms, including air, land and water.

Bipedalism—The ability of a mammal to walk on only two legs, considered to be one of the distinguishing characteristics of humans.

Brachiopod—A class of invertebrates having a bi-valve shell and two "arms" with tentacles by which they gather food.

Cenozoic Era—The time of "new life," for the emergence of a new kind of animal called the mammal (represented by a green strip on the Clock of Eons).

Cephalopods—Any of a class of mollusks, or soft-bodied invertebrates. Includes the squid, octopus, and cuttlefish.

Chordata—Animals with a notochord or spinal cord to organize their nervous system. Includes all vertebrates and some invertebrates, or transitional animals that have notochords without the protection of a vertebral column of bone.

Chromosphere—The outer layer of gases lying above the photosphere of the Sun. It is about 10,000 km thick but can only be seen during a solar eclipse because of the overwhelming brightness of the photosphere.

Clock of Eons—A teaching device in the shape of a clock, with different colored sections representing the time of pre-life and the various phases of life that have emerged since the formation of Earth. Used for storytelling and a timeline for the Story of Life.

Clovis—A group of Paleo "Indians" in America who were big game hunters, named for their distinctive, fluted spear points found in Clovis, NM.

Composition of the Earth—The part of the Montessori geography curriculum that deals with the layers of air, water, rock, and minerals that make up the planet Earth.

Cosmic Task—The unique contribution that anything in the Universe can make to the survival of the whole and the promotion of evolution.

Cosmogenesis—The sense in which evolution can be understood not only as *biogenesis*, but more broadly as the evolutionary birth and unfolding of the Universe and all its parts. A word of Greek origin meaning "universe-birth."

Cosmos—A Greek-derived word for the Universe, with the added connotation of an ordered whole.

Creation Story—The impressionistic lesson which tells the Story of the Universe and introduces studies in astronomy, physics, and chemistry. One of the five Great Lessons of the classic Montessori curriculum.

Crinoid—Lily-shaped class of echinoderms, or invertebrates that usually have a five-part bodily symmetry.

Cultural Curriculum—The subjects within the Montessori curriculum that have to do with passing on to later generations the accumulated wisdom of past "cultures"; an integrated blend of history, geography, biology, and physical science.

Directress (Director) — The term often used to describe the Montessori teacher, emphasizing that her/his job is not to *teach* information so much as to *guide or direct* the children into an area of study by stimulating their imagination and interest.

Ecozoic Era — A term used by Brian Swimme and Thomas Berry to describe the time when humans will abandon their exploitation of the resources of the Earth in favor of a mutual benefit and respect for the natural order of the world.

Élan Vital — The term used by French philosopher Henri Bergson (and adopted by Maria Montessori) for the "vital urge" that ensures the survival of life and carries evolution forward.

Eukaryotes — Living cells with a fully formed nucleus. Includes all of the kingdoms of life except the prokaryotes.

Evolution — The process of change through time; can be applied to the Universe (cosmogenesis) or, more commonly, to the emergence of various species of living organisms from their ancestors (biogenesis).

First Classification — The part of the Montessori biology curriculum that deals with the classification of the five kingdoms, at a level designed for use by the lower elementary children.

Folsom — A group of Paleo "Indians" in America who were big game hunters, named for their distinctive spear points found in Folsom, NM.

Foraminiferans — An order of tiny marine animals whose shells are generally perforated with minute holes (hence the name "hole-bearers").

Frontal Cortex — The upper front part of the brain that is considered to be the site of rational processing and thinking.

Fungi — One of the five kingdoms in a classification system that also includes Prokaryotes (Monera), Protoctista (Protista), Animals, and Plants.

Gaia — A mythological name given to the Earth by scientists to emphasize the organic balance of its systems such as water and air, and the interdependence of all its parts for survival of the whole.

Galaxy—A formation of billions of stars, usually organized into a spiral or elliptical shape through the opposing forces of gravity and centrifugal force, as nebula or enormous clouds of gas coalesced into stars.

Geneticist—A scientist who specializes in genetics, or the branch of biology dealing with heredity.

Gondwanaland—The name geologists give to the land mass including South America, Africa, India, Antarctica, and Australia that formed about 125 million years ago with the breakup of Pangaea.

Gravettians—A Paleolithic people who lived in eastern Europe, learned how to construct man-made houses and left behind intriguing statuettes of buxom female figures called "Venuses."

Great Lessons—Five key presentations in the classic Montessori curriculum that Mario Montessori at times referred to as "great lessons," emphasizing the content, and at other times as "great stories," emphasizing the form of presentation. Includes the Creation Story, the Story of Life, the Story of Humans, the Story of Math, and the Story of Language.

Great River—The impressionistic lesson used to introduce students to the study of human biology.

Hadean Eon—The time that was so "hellish" with crashing asteroids and exploding volcanoes that there was no life on Earth (from 4.5 billion years ago to 3.8 billion years ago). The first hours of the Clock of Eons, colored in black.

Hohokam—A group of Archaic "Indians" who were among the first farmers in North America and who are credited with developing irrigation to farm in the southwest deserts.

Homeostasis—The tendency of a living organism to achieve equilibrium through inner adjustment and self-regulation in response to changes in the outer world.

Hominid—A primitive ape resembling humans and thought to be descended from a common ancestor which eventually produced humans.

Homo erectus—This so-called "erect human" came after *Homo habilis* and lived in Africa from about a million years ago to about 200,000 years ago; *Homo erectus* is credited with the domestication of fire.

Homo habilis—The first identifiable species of true humans, associated with tool-making and living in East Africa from about two and a half million years ago to about one million years ago.

Homology—Similarity of structure, regardless of function, due to descent from a common ancestor.

Hopewell—A group of Archaic "Indians" who lived in the Ohio and Mississippi Valley and who followed the Adena as mound-builders. They also developed farming in the area.

Horme—A Greek word signifying the vital urge of survival, related to a life-related goal or contribution to the Universe, what Maria Montessori referred to as a "cosmic task."

Hydrotropism—The tendency of plants to grow their roots in a direction that will make them more accessible to water.

Igneous—The type of rocks formed by the solidification of molten magma.

Impressionistic Lessons—The term used to describe Montessori lessons or presentations with a high dramatic content designed to introduce an overview of a content area while inspiring students to further study.

Invertebrates—Animals without a backbone. The terminology has been replaced in many modern biology studies by "non-chordates" to distinguish them from animals with a notochord, with or without bony vertebrae.

Kitchen Midden Folk—People of the Mesolithic period who lived in present-day Denmark and who left behind huge mounds of shells from oysters and other shellfish.

Laurasia—The land mass including North America, Europe, and most of Asia that broke off from Pangaea about 125 million years ago.

GLOSSARY

Light Years—The distance light travels in one Earth year, or 5.9 trillion miles. Primarily a measurement of distance, but also an expression of time in that when we view a spot in the Universe a light year away, we are actually "seeing" that spot as it was a year ago.

Limbic System—The part of the brain that surrounds the brain stem and that is considered to be the center of emotions.

Long Black Line—A spool of black yarn with a small piece of red at the end, used in the Montessori history/biology curriculum to tell an initial version of the Story of Life.

Macrocosmic—Of the order of gigantic sizes, as opposed to microscopic; relating to the realm of the Universe, as opposed to the world of the atom.

Magdalenians—A Paleolithic culture of people from southwest France and northern Spain who used high-tech stone-age tools like harpoons and the atlatl spear-thrower.

Maglemosians—People of the Mesolithic period who lived in the swampy bogs of northern Europe and who invented the first true axe with a handle. They are also thought to have been the first people to adopt dogs as pets and helpers.

Mesolithic—A Greek-derived word meaning "middle stone age."

Mesozoic Era—The time of "middle life," when plants and animals moved onto the land and when amphibians and reptiles dominated the planet (represented in brown on the Clock of Eons).

Metamorphic—The type of rocks transformed into crystalline structures by extreme compression and heat.

Mitochondria—The part of the cell within the cytoplasm believed to process energy for the rest of the cell.

Mneme—A Greek word Montessori used for ontological and historical memory, or the part of identity which comes from ancestry in the broadest sense of that term.

Nautiloid—Marine animals having a spiral chambered shell.

Neolithic—A Greek-derived word meaning "new stone age," and used for the period when humans invented agriculture and began to live in villages.

Neozoic Era—The time of "newest life," when humans began to inhabit the Earth (represented by a thin red strip on the Clock of Eons).

Noosphere—A Greek-derived term coined by paleontologist Pierre Teilhard de Chardin to signify the emergence of human consciousness or the sphere of the Spirit.

Omega Point—Teilhard de Chardin's term for a time in the future when evolution will take the next major step forward through an integration of all humans into a single unity of Spirit.

Paleoanthropologist—A scientist who studies prehistoric humans in their physical structure and cultural lifestyles.

Paleolithic—A Greek-derived word meaning "old stone age," and used for the period when humans first developed the ability to turn stone into tools and weapons.

Paleontologist—A scientist who studies the life of past geological periods, principally through fossil evidence.

Paleozoic Era—The time of "old life," when multicellular plants and animals evolved in the seas (represented in blue on the Clock of Eons).

Pangaea—The supercontinent, or single land mass containing all the present continents, that geologists believe existed about 200 million years ago.

Panthalassa—The single ocean that surrounded Pangaea about 200 million years ago.

Periodic Table—An arrangement of chemical elements into tabular form according to their properties and behavior.

Phanerozoic Eon—The final two hours on the Clock of Eons, when the whole range of multi-cellular organisms evolved, up to and including humans. This eon is further divided into subdivisions called Eras.

Photosphere—The visible surface of the Sun, made up of a layer of gases about 5,000 km deep.

Photosynthesis—The formation of food as carbohydrates in the chlorophyll-containing cells of plants through the capture of the energy from the Sun.

Phototropism—The tendency of plants to grow their shoots and leaves in a direction to make them more accessible to light.

Phylum (pl. Phyla)—The largest divisions within each kingdom of living organisms, classified according to presumed common ancestry.

Planes of Development—The Montessori terminology for the four major stages of development she identified from birth to full adulthood: 0–6, 6–12, 12–18, and 18–24 years of age.

Prokaryotes—One of the five divisions in the five-kingdom classification system, also known as Monera, and including the most primitive living creatures whose cells don't yet have a well-defined nucleus (primarily bacteria).

Proterozoic Eon—The time of "first life" as we know it, when true, eukaryotic cells were formed (from 2.5 billion years ago to 543 million years ago). Represented in yellow on the Clock of Eons.

Protoctista—One of the five kingdoms in the classification of living things, also known as Protista, and including the simplest, mostly one-celled, living creatures with a defined nucleus but not having the clear characteristics of either plant or animal.

Ramapithecus—An extinct hominid, or human-like creature, of which only jaw bones were first discovered in India. The root word "pithecus" comes from the Greek word for ape, while "Rama" refers to an Indian god.

Sedimentary—The type of rocks formed from sediments or tiny fragments of mineral materials.

Sensitive Periods—A Montessori term for those times in a child's life when certain skills are most easily acquired because of the stage of their development and natural readiness for learning.

Sextillion—A sextillion is the number 1, followed by 21 zeros, or 10 to the power of 21.

Solutreans—A Paleolithic culture of people who lived in France after the Aurignacians and who are believed to have invented such technological advances as laurel leaf-shaped spear points and needles with an eye for threading.

Speciation—The evolutionary process by which species are formed.

Stellar Nucleosynthesis—The ability of stars to fuse or force together the nuclei of simple atoms into new, more complicated elements of the periodic table.

Sun and Earth Studies—The part of the Montessori geography curriculum that deals with the relationship between the Sun and Earth to produce night and day, the four seasons, and the time zones we have created.

Supernova—As gravity draws new matter into a giant star, astronomers say the pent-up energy eventually reaches a point where it explodes in a massive outburst called a supernova, producing all of the heavier elements in the periodic table and spewing the products of this fusion process out into surrounding space.

Taxonomy—The arrangement of animals, plants, and other living organisms into groups and sub-groups according to their relationships and shared characteristics.

Timelines—Representations, usually in linear fashion, of the passage of time, with a depiction of significant events.

Timeline of Life—The materials used in the Montessori history curriculum for telling the Story of Life and allowing students to explore and study biogenesis. This is one of the so-called "great lessons" in the curriculum, and the materials are used for story, timeline, and study.

Trilobites—Extinct marine arthropods, or jointed-limbed invertebrates, that lived during the Paleozoic Era and were characterized by three segments or lobes on their bodies.

Upper Paleolithic—An archeological term, with "upper" signifying "most recent" in the strata of a dig, "paleo" meaning "old," and "lithic" coming from the Greek word for "stone." Hence, it signifies the most recent part of the old Stone Age.

Vital Functions—The part of the Montessori biology curriculum that deals with the vegetative functions of nutrition, respiration, and circulation; the outside relationship functions of the nervous and skeletal-muscular systems; and reproduction.

Work of Wind and Water—The part of the Montessori geography curriculum that deals with the effects of the movement of air and the cycle of water on the planet Earth.

References

Bergson, Henri (1944). *Creative Evolution.* New York: Random House.

Berry, Thomas (1988). *The Dream of the Earth.* San Francisco: Sierra Club Books.

Berry, Thomas (1999). *The Great Work: Our Way into the Future.* New York: Bell Tower.

Bruning, R. H., Schraw, G. J. and Ronning, R. R. (1999). *Cognitive Psychology and Instruction.* Upper Saddle River, NJ: Prentice Hall.

Chattin-McNichols, John (1992). *The Montessori Controversy.* Albany, NY: Delmar Publishers.

Coles, Robert (1997). *The Moral Intelligence of Children,* New York: Random House.

Darwin, Charles (1979). *The Origin of Species.* New York: Gramercy House.

Darwin, Charles (1997). *The Descent of Man.* Amherst, NY: Prometheus Books.

Filkin, David (1997). *Stephen Hawking's Universe: The Cosmos Explained.* New York: Basic Books.

Goleman, D. (1995). *Emotional Intelligence.* New York: Bantam Books.

Gould, Stephen Jay (1991). *The Flamingo's Smile: Reflections in Natural History.* New York: W. W. Norton & Co.

Gould, Stephen Jay (1991). *Bully for Brontosaurus: Reflections in Natural History.* New York: W. W. Norton & Co.

Grazzini, Camillo (1997). "Cosmic Education at the Elementary Level and the Role of the Materials." *The NAMTA Journal*, Vol. 22 (1).

Honegger Fresco, Grazia (2000). *Montessori: perche no? Una pedagogia per la crescita.* Milan, Italy: FrancoAngeli.

Johanson, Donald and Edey, Maitland (1981). *Lucy — the Beginnings of Humankind.* New York: Warner Books.

John Paul II, Pope (1996). Message to Pontifical Academy of Sciences, October 22, 1996. Vatican City: Catholic Information Network.

Kahn, David (1998). "The Kodaikanal Experience: Kahn-Montessori Interview." *The NAMTA Journal*, 23 (2), Spring. Reprint of an article that first appeared in the *NAMTA Quarterly*, Fall 1979.

Kramer, Rita (1976). *Maria Montessori, a Biography.* Chicago: University of Chicago Press.

Levine, Joseph and Suzuki, David (1993). *The Secret of Life: Redesigning the Living World.* Toronto: Stoddart Publishing.

Lillard, Paula Polk (1996). *Montessori Today: A Comprehensive Approach to Education form Birth to Adulthood.* New York: Schocken Books.

Margulis, Lynn (1988). *Five Kingdoms: An Illustrated Guide to the Phyla of Life on Earth.* New York: W. H. Freeman.

Montessori, Maria (1973). *To Educate the Human Potential.* Madras, India: Kalakshetra Publications.

Montessori, Maria (1989). *The Child, Society and the World: Unpublished Speeches and Writings.* Oxford, England: Clio Press.

Montessori, Maria (1992). *Education and Peace,* Oxford, England: Clio Press.

Montessori, Maria (1994). *From Childhood to Adolescence.* Oxford, England: Clio Press.

Montessori, Mario (1998). "The Impact of India." *The NAMTA Journal*, 23 (2). Reprint of an article that first appeared in the 1969/70 issue of *Around the Child,* the publication of the Association of Montessorians — Calcutta.

Montessori, Mario M., Jr. (1976). *Education for Human Development: Understanding Montessori.* New York: Schocken Books.

Piaget, Jean (1997). *The Moral Judgment of the Child,* New York: Free Press.

Rambusch, Nancy McCormick (1992). "Montessori in America: A History." In Loeffler, Margaret Howard (editor), *Montessori in Contemporary American Culture.* Portsmouth, NH: Heinemann.

Resnick, Mike (1982). *Birthright: The Book of Man.* New York: Farthest Star.

Sagan, Carl (1980). *Cosmos.* New York: Random House.

Sagan, Carl and Druyan, Ann (1992). *Shadows of Forgotten Ancestors: A Search for Who We Are.* New York: Random House.

Standing, E. M. (1957). *Maria Montessori: Her Life and Work.* New York: New American Library.

Swimme, Brian and Berry, Thomas (1992). *The Universe Story: from the Primordial Flaring Forth to the Ecozoic Era—a Celebration of the Unfolding of the Cosmos.* San Francisco: Harper.

Teilhard de Chardin, Pierre (1975). *The Phenomenon of Man.* New York: Harper & Row.

Wolf, Aline D. (1996). *Nurturing the Spirit.* Hollidaysburg, PA: Parent Child Press.

ABOUT THE AUTHORS

Michael and D'Neil Duffy have been involved in Montessori education since 1973, when their daughter entered a New York Montessori school at the age of 2½. D'Neil, who had been a teacher in the traditional public and private schools for 12 years, fell in love with the Montessori method and philosophy. She took her primary level training with the Association Montessori Internationale in Atlanta. After teaching in other schools for several years, she founded the Blackstock Montessori School in Villa Rica, GA, in 1979 and went on to get her 6–12 elementary certification from the American Montessori Society through the Center for Montessori Teacher Education in New York. D'Neil taught at primary and both elementary levels, and she was the administrator of Blackstock Montessori for 21 years. She also served one term on the AMS board.

Michael, who had been a journalist by profession, got his AMS 6–12 elementary certification through CMTE/NY and joined the Blackstock Montessori School in 1989, teaching in the lower, then upper elementary classes. Both became trainers in the elementary teacher-training program at CMTE/NY, and they have trained teachers in New York, Phoenix, Boston, Toronto, Vancouver, and Puerto Rico with CMTE/NY and other training centers. In 2013, the Duffys helped launch the Montessori Elementary Teacher Training Collaborative (METTC), which has taken over the role of elementary training from CMTE/NY.

The Duffys have also given workshops at national and international Montessori conferences, as well as related organizations such as the International Big History Association, and their work has been published in Montessori magazines. They have authored three books on Montessori education. Besides this book, Michael authored *Math Works: Montessori Math and the Developing Brain*, and they co-authored *Love of Learning: Supporting Intrinsic Motivation in Montessori Students*. All three were originally published through Parent Child Press, now a division of Montessori Services.

In addition to their Montessori credentials, both have masters degrees in education, D'Neil with a specialty in Guidance and Counseling, and Michael with a specialty in Media Education. They retired from Blackstock in 2001 to devote more of their time to teacher-training, writing, and educational consulting, and they have moved to the mountains of Virginia to be within a day's drive of their four grandchildren, all of them in Montessori schools.